How to Write a Retail Store Business Plan in Ten Steps
Business Plan Sample and Template Included

Table of Contents

Acknowledgments

The drive and determination to write this short novel were in no small part due to my wonderful wife, Tishauna, kids, Cara, Katy, Maggie, and Paul Jr., stepson, Jayden, and parents.

About the Author

Paul Borosky, MBA., Doctoral Candidate, is the owner of Quality Business Plan, Tutor4Finance, Enjoy Florida Today, and FinanceHomeworkHelp.net. His time is mostly spent with his family, business plan writing, writing books, financial modeling, and cruising. Oh, so many cruises.

Paul's first run-in with finance was as a mortgage broker in the mid-1990s. His fascination with finance led to an MBA with numerous credits in different finance courses. Recently, he has created two finance curriculums for a local college and is considered a subject matter expert in finance.

Currently, Paul is completing his dissertation, writing business plans, tutoring finance to students the world over, and teaching finance for a local college. In the future, he intends to write extensively related to business plans, vacationing, strategic planning, corporate finance, and incorporating financial modeling into the startup and expanding organizations.

Introduction

As a professional business consultant and business plan writer, I am often asked by entrepreneurs, "What is the first step to starting a retail store business?"

When I first started out as a business consultant, I would explain to my client their place in the entrepreneurial process. I then support this analysis with proven academic and practicing business theory, along with recommending specific steps to start or expand their retail store operations.

After going through this process time and time again with retail store entrepreneurs, it dawned on me that the first step I ALWAYS recommend is writing a business plan.

Unfortunately, most retail store entrepreneurs do not know how to write a professionally polished and structured business plan. Hell, most owners don't know how to write any type of business plan at all. Because of this systemic issue, I decided to write this book focused on a ten-step process for writing a well-structured business plan.

The retail store business plan writing steps include all aspects of the business plan writing process, beginning with developing an executive summary to constructing a polished funding request.

In each step, I introduce you to a different business plan section. Next, I explain, in layman's terms, what the section means, offer a retail store-specific business plan sample, and analyze the example to help you understand it. The objective of this detailed process is to ensure a full understanding of each segment, with the goal of you being able to write a professional retail store business plan for yourself, by yourself!

IF you still need help writing your business plan, at the end of the book, I ALSO supply you with a professionally written sample retail store business plan AND a retail store business plan template for you to use. To put a proverbial cherry on top, **I have conducted and included preliminary retail store market research for you** to use in your personalized plans!

In the end, I am supremely confident that this book, with its numerous tools and tips, will help you develop a retail store business plan to fit your individual needs.

Step 1 – Retail store Description

The company description section of a business plan should thoroughly explain, in a nutshell, what the retail store will do, how the firm will do it, where the retail store will do it, and specific strategies that may, or may not, be used through the course of operations.

This sounds like a lot of information for just one section. And yes, it definitely is. This section, just about, is the only one devoted to thoroughly describing the inner workings of the company.

Retail Store Summary:

The leadoff batter for this section is the retail store summary. The purpose of a company summary is to give the reader a broad understanding of the organization. To accomplish this feat, make sure to answer the questions: who, what, where, when, and how, in one or two paragraphs.

Business Plan Writing Tip:

When writing the retail store company summary, try to keep the section's content to a paragraph or two. Keep in mind; a business plan is a tool used for documenting the proposed business. However, due to internal and external forces in a retail store's environment (new products, competitors, etc.), providing too many details may lead to a plan that needs continuous updating.

A better practice, at least when starting up a retail store, is to leave some wiggle room for changes. The best way to do this is to keep the scope of writing broad. In other words, provide enough details so the reader understands the business, but not so many elements that the plan needs updating more than once every six months.

Sample:

Retail Store Summary

ABC Retail store will be a limited liability corporation located at 123 Broadway St. in Orlando, FL. Our business owner(s) will be John Smith. Our retail store's main product line will be clothing. To complement our clothing lines, we will also offer jewelry, shoes, hats, and gloves. Our hours of operation will be from 8 AM To 8:30 PM, seven days a week.

Analysis:

The structure above succinctly shows the name of the company, the type of legal structure for the business, products offered, location, and hours of operation. In other words, who, what, where, when, and how. Further, the information is kept to a paragraph. Short and sweet.

Competitive Advantages:

The competitive advantage for a company is what the firm will do better than other competitors. As with most sections of the business plan, this concept may be interpreted in a multitude of ways. To illustrate, a competitive advantage may include differentiated retail product offerings, a prime location, or even an exceptional customer service staff.

Business Plan Writing Tip:

Think about how the firm will be different from local competitors. Once you identify and state the differentiating factor, or factors, then explain why this is important for the business or to the customers.

Sample:

Competitive Advantages

ABC company will have specific competitive advantages once our firm starts operations. First, our retail store will sell high-quality, name-branded products from companies that have pledged to embrace eco-friendly practices. No other retail store in the area has committed to this business model. Further, our firm will adopt the "full-attire" concept in our product offerings. For our full-attire idea, we will employ knowledgeable associates that can help customers match clothing with accessories to create unique looks based on our customer's tastes.

Analysis:

The first competitive advantage should always be the most critical competitive advantage for the organization. When discussing this competitive advantage, make sure to explain, in detail, what the competitive advantage is and why it's essential. Also, be detailed but concise.

Also, touch on one or two competitive advantages, but no more. The business plan should show some differentiation, but the distinction should not seem too far outside of the norm. In other words, there are proven business models out there, use them and differentiate, but don't differentiate too much.

Product Description:

In the product description section, make sure to thoroughly explain the product(s) the retail store will offer. To illustrate, a store owner may list inventory items and brand names. An inventory item could be a "shirts," and brands may be Polo, Nike, and Under Armour. By doing this, the readers of the business plan will fully understand the products and scope of the business.

Business Plan Writing Tip:

Try not to exceed four or five product categories. Granted, a business plan should be thorough in this section. However, always keep in mind, the business plan should be balanced as well. Try not to have one part outweigh, in word-content, all of the other segments in the business plan. If the product offerings exceed five or six items, include the rest in an appendix.

Sample:

Product Description

Shirts
Our shirts product lines may include Polo, Under Armour, Nike, and other named brand companies dedicated to offering high-quality shirt products and supports corporate social responsibility.

Pants:
The pants product line will focus on brand names like Levi's, St. John, and Ralph Lauren. As for type, we will carry straight leg, Ultraflex, and boot cut.

Accessories:
To round out any outfit, we will carry a wide selection of sunglasses, jewelry, shoes, and other items that may be trending or in high demand for customers.

For a full product selection, please review Appendix A.

Analysis:

I chose to identify products like shirts, pants, and accessories. Under each subcategory, I briefly explained the possible product selections. The objective here is to help the reader understand likely inventory items that may be offered.

Pricing Strategy:

The pricing strategy section in a business plan should explain the business owner's thoughts and ideas about how their prices compare to competitors. Popular pricing strategies may include low-cost leader, premium pricing, and the best value pricing approach.

The low-cost leader pricing approach is when products or services are priced slightly below local or regional retail stores. An excellent example of a low-cost leader would be Walmart.

As for premium pricing, this would be when the business owner charges higher prices than area competitors, such as Macy's. Often times, higher prices are justified due to differentiated services or higher quality product lines.

In my most humble of opinions, my favorite pricing strategy, by far, is the best value approach. For this strategy, the management team will continually research the prices of comparable products offered by competitors in the area. From this research, the retail store owner will then create a base price for each product using the averages of competitors in the area. Next, the organization will make price item adjustments based on the quality of the product or overall retail store reputation as compared to yours. The end objective is to have all of your product items priced competitively.

Business Plan Writing Tip:

When selecting a pricing strategy, make sure to use a financial model. By using a financial model, a business owner can see the impact price changes may have on customer volume and net profits.

Pricing Strategy Example			
Item	Low Cost	Premium	Best Value
Number of Customers	100	50	75
Average Product Price	22.00	35.00	30.00
Total Revenues	2,200.00	1,750.00	2,250.00
COGS	770.00	612.50	787.50
Gross Profit	1,430.00	1,137.50	1,462.50

In the example above, there are three different pricing strategies: low-cost, premium, and best value. Based on the financial model created, it looks like the best value approach will net you the highest profits, even though the sales price is lower than premium pricing.

Sample:

Pricing Strategy

Our pricing structure will be focused on the best value strategy. For this strategy, our management team will continually research the prices of clothing lines offered by local retail store competitors in the area. From this research, we will create base inventory item prices using the averages of competitors in the area. Next, our organization will make product item price adjustments based on the quality of the clothing line, the ambiance of the competitors' establishment, and overall clothing line selection as compared to ours. The end objective is to have all of our products prices competitively priced using the best value strategic model.

Analysis:

This sample shows the business owner embracing the best value strategic pricing approach. Also, it emphasizes a specific strategy for implementing its pricing practice. The result is a well thought out strategy, which addresses the pricing segment need of a business plan, as well as, allows for understanding the thought process behind the strategic pricing action.

Business Models:

One of my favorite sections to write in any business plan is the business model section. This is because a business model can be just about any action or process that makes retail store money. From this, business model sections vary significantly between retail stores.

Popular sections in my retail store business model category may include discussions about clothes line quality, hours of operation, number of workers, customer experience, or even the business owner's philosophy with treating employees and suppliers.

Business Plan Writing Tip:

When writing about business models, make sure to first identify the business model. Then discuss how the business model will operate. By doing this, retail store owners can show how different aspects of their operation will impact their profits and or benefit customers.

Sample:

Business Models

Operations:

Our operational structure will seek to achieve a high-end retail store's breadth of product selections while offering access to knowledgeable attendants. As a customer approaches our retail store, they will be met with advertising decals on the door and smiling attendants at the entrance. This will allow visitors to feel at home while they shop for their clothing needs. At the counter, our visitors will be offered complimentary products and accessories to their purchases. This will ensure a complete wardrobe makeover after each visit.

Hours of Operations:

Our hours of operations business model will be structured to ensure our retail store customers' needs are met at a convenient time. From this, our organization will be open from 8 AM to 8:30 PM, seven days a week.

Analysis:

The example above is based on a general retail store operation. Specifically, the perspective used in the business model example was from the customer. By including the customer's perspective of operations, an owner can describe the customer's experience and show why the operational structure has been created and the desired experience anticipated.

As for hours of operation, personally, I like to address this segment in the business model section, as well. The strategy is used to keep operational business components in one section.

Location:

The location section of the business plan will be structured differently, depending on the industry. Usually, in the location section, I will first note the retail store's address. Once this is done, then a discussion about the inherent benefits of the location should be addressed. For example, make sure to discuss square footage, usage of the square footage, and layout of the site. Once complete, next examine the external benefits of the location. Outside benefits may include parking availability, proximity to your target market demographics, and distance from major thoroughfares.

Business Plan Writing Tip:

For most of my business plans, I prefer to include a map picture with the location address labeled. This helps to emphasize the external benefits of the location.

Sample:

Location

As previously stated, our location will be in the Orlando, Florida, area. The proposed location size will be about 4,500 square feet. Approximately three-quarters of the area will be dedicated to the shopping space for customers. The rest of the area will be devoted to the back of the house operations like storage, office space, and packaging.

As for competition, this area has few other high-end clothing retail stores within a several miles radius. This will enable us to capture a significant portion of the casual retail market in the area.

Analysis:

For my business plans, I like to label this subsection header in bold font. This helps the retail store owner, or other readers, scan through the document and identify important pieces of information. Next, I always include the city and state, at a minimum, for the location. If a location has not been found, then the owner should outline the parameters needed for their operation. For this example, the company needs approximately 4,500 ft.^{2} and the ability to divide the facility between the front of house operations and office space, packaging space, and storage.

The final component of the location section I usually address is competition. A caveat; if there is a saturation of competitors in the area, I may skip over this component or explain why the selected location is best suited for the area.

Future Plans:

The future plan section should contain a discussion about the retail store owner's thoughts and ideas for the future. The views may include expanding operations to new locations or adding new product items. A popular discussion topic in this section is about opening a second or third location in the region. Regardless of the firm's future plans, make sure to show a conceptual strategy for growth.

Business Plan Writing Tip:

My preference is to be somewhat ambiguous with future growth plans. For example, a retail store owner may plan to open 4 or 5 new locations within the next five years. In this situation, explain in your plan that the retail store will expand to several new locations within this timeframe. This shows that there are growth expectations. However, a specific number of new operations are held back.

Sample:

Future Plans

Within the next 24 months, our firm will open new locations in the Orlando / Central Florida area. The new sites and timeframe will be based on funding, leadership availability, and other factors. Further, our management team will introduce new product items within the next 12 months. These items will be selected based on customer demand, how well the items complement our current offering and the availability of the products.

Analysis:

Notice that a specific timeframe is stated. This allows the business owner to set a deadline for when the expansion should be completed. Next, if the future plans include expansion, identify the general area in which the retail store may grow. This helps to set specific parameters for geographic development. In this case, growing in the Central Florida area shows the business owner is seeking to exploit brand recognition in one particular centralized location.

Business Objectives and Timeline:

Every business will have specific objectives they wish to achieve. To accomplish the coveted objectives, retail store owners need to list the objectives and have a specific deadline for completion. What better way to categorize a list of objectives than to put them in a timeline?

By following this structure, not only will a retail store owner be able to identify the objectives they need to accomplish, but the timeframe and order in which the objectives should be conquered.

Business Plan Writing Tip:

For this section, I like to break up the timeline into three to six-month brackets. Further, when writing this section, I almost always start by developing the last time slot first. If my business objectives and timeline will cover up to two years, then I would start with a two-year point and work to the present. By following this strategy, the business owner can make sure each business objective aligns with the others.

Sample:

Business Objectives and Timeline

> ### 1 - 3 Months
> - Obtain investor funding.
> - Identify the facility and negotiate a rental agreement.
> - Engage in buildout activities.
> - Open for business.
>
> ### 3 – 6 Months
> - Start an advertising campaign.
> - Evaluate marketing strategy and implement it.
> - Evaluate business models.
>
> ### 6 – 12 Months
> - Optimize marketing strategies.

- Optimize business models.
- Examine external environment for market opportunities.

Analysis:

In the example above, I staggered the time frames between three months to six-month sections. The further out I went, timewise, the broader the timeframe. This is because almost all objectives past six months should be broad due to the continual fluctuation of market activities. In other words, stuff changes too much in business to have specific objectives past six months.

In contrast, for the first six months, try to be as specific as possible. As shown above, for the first three months, I have specific objectives listed in the order that they should be achieved. This helps the retail store owner stay focused on a sequential set of tasks for the short-term.

Mission Statement:

The mission statement section of the business plan should succinctly describe what a retail store will do to earn their revenues. Some retail store owners like to focus on customer service as a center of their mission statement. Others prefer discussing the quality of the products sold. Regardless, the mission statement needs to convey the retail store owner's philosophy or mindset related to operations or customer service.

Business Plan Writing Tip:

The mission statement should be short enough so employees and customers will remember it. For my business's mission statement, I chose to focus on helping small business owners achieve their objectives.

Sample:

Mission Statement

"Our retail store's mission is to provide the best name brand selections in a friendly atmosphere and clean environment."

Analysis:

The sample started with identifying the retail store's primary offering, which is a high-end name brand products. Next, the mission described the atmosphere they wish customers to enjoy, while at their establishment. This shows that the retail store will strive to continuously improve their products while ensuring a predetermined ambiance for their guests.

Vision Statement:

The vision statement for a business plan focuses on how a retail store will look in the distant future. Organizations may take a few different approaches to write a vision statement. In the first approach, the statement may include the number of employees at that point in time, the geographic area serviced by the business, or brand recognition for the retail store. In most instances, the timeframe is dated 3 to 5 years into the future.

A second method is to forgo a specific time frame and focus on an "impossible" vision. The impossible vision helps retail store owners and employees continually strive to meet exceedingly high expectations.

Business Plan Writing Tip:

Selecting the vision statement format is pretty much a retail store owners' preference. If a specific timeframe is used, then the vision may need to be updated periodically. For an 'impossible' vision, this type of statement is, more or less, static.

Sample:

Vision Statement

"Deliver world-class wardrobe changes using named brand products on a global level."

Analysis:

For this vision statement, I chose the "impossible" vision route. What I mean by an impossible vision is that objectively speaking, there is no way that a retail store will accomplish the stated vision. However, from a motivational perspective, this overreaching vision will help keep the owner focused on expanding services to new areas.

Value Statement:

The value statement should highlight specific values the retail store owner and employees embrace and practice on an unremitting basis. In this section, use bullet points to convey the values for the retail store.

Business Plan Writing Tip:

This segment is pretty straightforward. Popular values may be honesty, high quality, technological innovation.

Sample:

Value Statement

- Honesty.
- Fair prices.
- Named brand clothing.
- Technical innovations

Analysis:

These values express the retail store owner's commitment to fairness and honest business practices. As a rule, try to keep the value statement short and to the point.

Keys to Success:

Most business plans finish off the company description section with a discussion about "Keys to Success." For this category, focus on the retail store owner's perspective as to critical actions for success. Common keys to success include customer service, employee equality, and innovation. Again, in this section, use either bullet points or a graphical representation.

Business Plan Writing Tip:

Use a graphical representation in the section to succinctly show thoughts and ideas about the actions or concepts that the retail store will embrace and is essential for its long-term success.

Sample:

Keys to Success

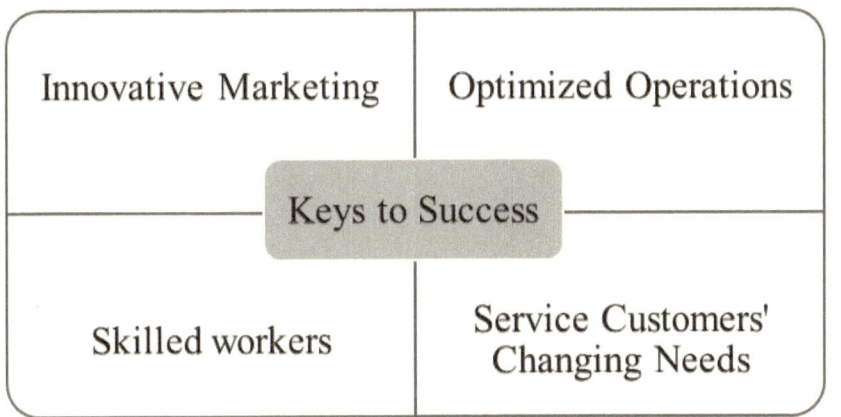

Analysis:

In the graphical representation, the star of the show is "Keys to Success." In each section, the key to success focused on a different aspect of the retail store. Innovative marketing related to marketing actions, optimized operations to the retail store's operational business models, etc. In other words, all keys to success are not focused on one area of the retail store, but a range of different aspects for the facility.

Step 2 – Target Market

The target market section of a business plan should concentrate on a specific demographic or group of people, with similar traits or characteristics that need or want the retail store's services. At least, this is the "textbook" definition of the target market.

When I have my client described their target market, I like to set a scene for the client. The scenario goes something like this:

"You see a person walking towards you. There is no doubt in your mind that this person will absolutely, 100%, unequivocally stop in your retail store. What does this person look like? Describe the person in as much detail as possible. "

Here are some helpful questions to answer.

- What does a person look like?
- Is the person male and female?
- Young or old?
- How are they dressed? Blue-collar worker? Executive? Office worker?

Once a retail store owner can identify their primary target market, they are now ready to complete the primary target market segment of the business plan.

On a final note, keep in mind, just because a retail store entrepreneur has a narrow target market, it does not mean that this demographic will be their only customers. The organization very well may have a broad appeal to a multitude of demographics. However, every retail store has a limited amount of resources they can dedicate to advertising. Because of the scarce resource, having a target market in mind who will best appeal to the retail store's advertising dollars is definitely advisable.

Primary Target Market:

Most retail stores will have several demographics that appeal to their product offerings and chosen theme. However, almost always, there is one demographic or group of people that will most definitely want the retail store's core product items. This demographic is the primary target market for the retail store.

Business Plan Writing Tip:

Make sure to describe the primary target market in detail. Also, justify why this demographic was selected. Not only will this help you understand whom the firm is targeting for their products, but why this group was selected.

Sample:

Primary Target Market

Our primary target market will be young, blue-collar works. Specifically, females between the ages of 25 to 35. This demographic was selected because of their propensity to enjoy named brand clothing while shopping in a comfortable environment.

Analysis:

The primary target market identified in this example were female, executive between the ages of 25 to 35, who enjoys named brand clothing while shopping in a comfortable environment. In this example, there is a specific age bracket, person description, and appreciation noted for the organization's products.

Just by reading these couple of sentences, a person can visualize what the target market looks like. As noted above again, just because the target market is a narrow group of people does not mean the organization will not appeal to other demographics.

Identifying the primary target market will allow the retail store owner to devise advertising campaigns that will appeal to this demographic. Further, a retail store owner can decorate their establishment using items and decor that will appeal to this demographic.

Secondary Target Market:

The secondary target market should be written in a similar manner as the primary target market. Except, a separate demographic should be constructed. By following this process, the retail store owner is showing that their facility will appeal to more than just one demographic. In other words, having a secondary target market indicates a broad appeal for the retail store's offerings.

Sample:

Secondary Target Market

As for the secondary target market, this will be medical professionals working at the hospital across the street or in medical facilities surrounding the hospital. This demographic was selected due to its proximity to our retail store.

Analysis:

In this example, a demographic was selected based on profession and geographic distance from our hypothetical retail store. This shows that the store will appeal to a wide array of people, as well as niche, targeted groups.

Target Market Growth Potential:

Target market growth is another key component that should be addressed in the target market section of the business plan. Target market growth potential is how much growth a retail store entrepreneur expects in their target market. Usually, this is measured in percentages or actual growth estimate numbers.

Business Plan Writing Tip:

When writing the target market growth potential segment of the business plan, I like to, personally, including a little bit of math. For example, if the executive level segment of the city is approximately 25,000 people, and the growth rate in the city has been 1.3% annually, we can then multiply the 25,000 by 1.013. This would give us a population target market 25,325 people in the next 12 months. This process may also be utilized in the same manner for subsequent years as well.

Sample:

Target Market Growth Potential

Based on research from website XYZ, the current executive-level workforce in ABC City is 25,000 people. The U.S. Census Bureau has noted that the city's population increased by 1.3% annually over the last five years. Based on this factor, our retail store owner expects a similar growth rate for the next five years. From this, the target market formulation will be 25,325 within the next 12 months. In two years, our target market population will expand to 25,655 people.

Analysis:

The important take away in the segment is that the retail store owner's assumptions, which are the population growth rate and the number of executive-level workers, are sourced. By showing where your information comes from, the entrepreneur is adding credibility to the assumptions. The math, obviously, stands for itself.

Step 3– Market Analysis

The market analysis section of the business plan should address and examine the external aspects of the retail store industry. Common external aspects of business would include the business's industry, competitor review, and possibly a discussion about the economy and its potential effects on the industry as a whole.

Industry Overview:

Identify the main industry the business competes, in this case, the retail store industry. Once the industry is identified, then try and determine if there are sub-industries, with enough data, that aligns with your retail concept. For example, in the retail store industry, subcategories include discount stores, high-end retail, and mixed usage (Walmart) establishments. With this done, now research and take notes about the statistics and trends, such as total industry sales, growth rates for the industry, and popular tends currently being exploited.

Business Plan Writing Tip:

Thoroughly describe the characteristics and trends in the industry. For example, in the retail store industry, common characteristics would be growth rates, the price range of the products, and new retail store themes like novelty items or same-day delivery.

Sample:

Family clothing stores cater to men, women, and children through a wide array of product offerings like shirts, pants, and trending accessories. This industry is expected to exceed $110 billion in sales next year. To support further growth, industry experts project between a 1% to 1.3% growth rate.

Analysis:

This example started with explaining the specific characteristics commonly displayed by competitors in the industry. Next, brief revenue and growth rate discussion of the overall industry was offered. This then led to addressing the potential revenues for the subsection industry, as well as the potential growth rate for the future.

Industry Statistics:

Industry statistics may focus on a wide array of topics. A great way to start the retail store statistic segment just does an internet search about the industry and its statistics. Once this is complete, start reading articles and taking notes about the industry and specific statistics.

In going through this process, not only will the business owner deepen their knowledge about the industry, but they will also be able to show, through writing, in-depth research was done on the topic.

Business Plan Writing Tip:

When writing this section, I prefer to use bullet points to show statistics about the retail store industry.

Sample:

Statistics

- Industry experts predict that athletic wear will outpace other product lines by over 50% for the next several years.

- Women's clothing sales are projected to encapsulate 50% of all clothing items sold.

- Brick-and-mortar retail establishments have been entering the online retail space to complement their services at a faster pace than previous years.

- Customers' tastes tend to change faster with apparel than with other mature industries.

Analysis:

This example shows various statistics in relation to the retail store industry. As you can see, the structure used is a bullet point format. To take it a step further, make sure to utilize footnotes for citations. This will add credibility to your statistics section.

Threats, Trends, and Opportunities:

The trends, threats, and opportunity section are an excellent opportunity for the retail store owner to show how "in tune" they are with customer trends, and industry opportunities. When I write this section for clients, I usually like to equalize the information with an even number of threats, trends, and opportunities. This shows a well-balanced and researched section.

Business Plan Writing Tip:

Even though "opportunities" is listed last in the title, I often start this section by discussing opportunities in the marketplace first. Opportunities in an industry may be found in a multitude of ways. Some retail store owners survey potential customers to find out their needs. Other business owners will network with regional or national competitors to identify industry opportunities. Regardless of how opportunities are identified, make sure to thoroughly explain your findings.

As for structure, I prefer to use paragraph form for addressing the threats, trends, and opportunities.

Sample:

Trends, Threats, and Opportunities

An important threat to the industry would be related to the overall economy. Currently, job growth and employment are at all-time-highs. From this, people have enough discretionary funds to afford high-end apparel. Unfortunately, in the event of an economic recession, as discretionary funds for people decrease, profits for the retail store industry may show a correlated effect.

As for an opportunity, high-end retail shoppers are increasing selecting "mom and pop" retail stores over retail chain locations due to better service and appealing product selections. This allows for startup retail stores to enter the market place and gain a loyal following. Finally, trends in the retail store industry may be found in technological innovations. Technological innovations may help retail store owners offer in-demand clothing lines or enhanced service for premium prices.

Analysis:

Each topic, trend, threat, and opportunity were given equal attention. Also, thorough explanations were provided to support each finding.

Keys to Success:

The industry "keys to success" section will be different as compared to the "keys to success" discussion found in the retail store description category. As noted in the retail store's description, the keys to success were written based on the business owner's perspective of the retail store. In contrast, the industry section keys to success use research, and the perspective employed should be from the retail store industry as a whole. In other words, what are most of your competitors doing, and doing well, in order to be successful in the industry?

Business Plan Writing Tip:

For this section, make sure to do research and take notes. When I write a key to success section for the industry, I often review articles related to industry leaders. As I go through the articles, I will jot down notes related to actions they have taken to be successful. After I have gone through several articles, I then compare the notes with the objective of finding commonalities. To illustrate, for retail stores, an important key to success is a themed presentation. Just look at Victoria Secret, Hollister, or American Eagle.

Sample:

Keys to Success

To be successful in the retail store industry, competitors need to focus on hiring skilled employees. In other words, small businesses must employ and retain qualified and well-trained workers. Qualifications may not necessarily be in traditional schooling. However, experience with apparel coordination, technology, and customer service is necessitated to ensure that a guest has a memorable visit to a retail store.

Analysis:

In this example, the keys to success were focused on a small business owner competing in the retail store industry. An important identification, based on industry research, was the need for skilled workers. With this as a foundation, a brief discussion as to why this fact was focused on was needed.

SWOT Analysis:

The SWOT analysis is a popular strategic tool used by retail store owners to quickly and broadly identify different aspects of the retail store's internal and external environments. Unfortunately, most retail store owners use the SWOT analysis incorrectly.

The SWOT analysis is broken up into four segments, which are strengths, weaknesses, opportunities, and threats. This is common knowledge for most small retail store owners. However, what most small business owners do not know is that the strengths and weaknesses are one category, and opportunities and threats are a second.

In the strength and weaknesses segment, the retail store owner should focus on the internal aspects of their business. What are the retail store's strengths and weaknesses? For the opportunities and threats section, this is where the owner examines its external environment, seeking out opportunities and potential threats to the organization.

Business Plan Writing Tip:

Make sure to use a visually appealing format, bullet points, and always, always have at least twice as many strengths and opportunities as compared to weaknesses and threats.

Sample:

Strengths
- Management experience.
- Documented plans
- Themed retail concept
- Training program

Weakness
- Startup retail store.
- Untested business location.

Opportunities
- Community involvement
- Appeal to a wide variety of clientele.
- Location
- Brand building

Threats
- Local competitors
- Susceptible to economic downturn.

Analysis:

Take note; the strength and weakness section focused on the internal aspects of the retail store. Whereas the opportunities and threats segments concentrated on the external environment.

Competitive Analysis:

The competitive analysis section is where the retail store owner has an opportunity to examine and discuss local or regional competitors. This section may be as short as listing competing retail stores, their distance from the target facility, and a paragraph summarizing the competitors' strengths and weaknesses. Or, this segment may be a full-blown competitive analysis analyzing important segments of each competitors' retail store operation. For most retail store owners, the former approach is often best.

Business Plan Writing Tip:

The competitive analysis section, in my most humble of opinions, should be short and sweet. The preferred structure that I use is to identify the competitor's name, address, hours of operation, and a website link. With this completed, I then analyze the competition from a customer's perspective. To do this, just review the competitor's website and Google/Facebook reviews about the retail store. In following this structure, the retail store owner is able to gain important perspectives as to how the competition operates and, potentially, their strengths and glaring weaknesses.

Sample:

Shop Here Retail Store is a "mom and pop" retail store in the Washington DC. area. The retail store was founded in 1984 and prides themselves on their 24hr availability (via online shopping opportunities). As for services, the retailer offers high-end women's' clothing, focused on business casual, sports, and eveningwear. Based on a Google search, customers have had mixed reviews. Most reviews seemed satisfied with the retailer's clothing quality and service. However, some past customers complained that the cleanliness of the facility was lacking.

Analysis:

The short paragraph above succinctly noted the name of the competitor, a brief background of the competitor, if available, and a short discussion related to how customers perceive the organization.

Step 4 – Organization and Management

The organization and management section should be used to discuss the business structure of the retail store, management team, and job responsibilities.

Management Summary:

In the management summary section, most retail store owners will include a brief bio of the founder and the management team. When writing the bio, make sure to highlight the skills and experiences that are associated with the retail store.

Business Plan Writing Tip:

Some retail store owners like to believe that their business is all about them. And for a lot of small retail stores, it is. However, view the egocentric approach from an investor perspective; if something happens to the retail store owner, then the investor may lose their investment because the business would not be able to continue.

Because of this important issue, try to keep the bio section at a paragraph or less for the founder. This is enough information to demonstrate experience and competence. But, not so much information that the retail store owner and management team become the star of the show as compared to the business.

Sample:

Owner Bio

John Smith, Sr., MBA., is the founder and CEO of ABC Retail store. He has started and managed numerous successful small retail stores over the last ten years. Retail stores started and managed, includes a high-end clothing store, athletic apparel location, and Walmart location. For each business, he was responsible for all aspects of the organization, from marketing to strategic planning.

Analysis:

The brief bio first identifies the person discussed and their job title. Following this introduction, a brief discussion about experiences was made. This showed the owner has qualifications for the new retail store and has supporting experiences as well.

Job Responsibilities:

The job responsibilities section is mainly included to help the retail store owner demonstrate an in-depth understanding of the retail store structure and document potential positions needed. Further, by discussing and identifying job responsibilities, the retail store owner can alleviate future disagreements between the executive team members. This is done by explicitly stating job responsibilities for the business owner, executive team members, and hourly staff.

Business Plan Writing Tip:

For larger retail stores, not all positions and job descriptions should be included. For example, a retail store job responsibility section might list the executive team positions, managers, shift leaders, stockers, and apparel coordinator positions. This indicates that the business owner has at least a basic knowledge of the different positions needed for the retail store.

Sample:

Job Positions and Responsibilities

CEO:
- Create and execute marketing strategies for retail store growth.
- Align retail store strategies with the vision statement.
- Negotiating contracts with vendors.
- Ensure legal compliance for the retail store.
- Continually examine the firm's external environment for new market opportunities.

General Manager:
- Control inventory to ensure optimal levels are attained.
- Manage day-to-day operations of the retail store.
- Assist stockers and apparel coordinators during high volume times.
- Interview and hire new employees.
- Assist in the onboarding process for new employees.

Analysis:

For each job position, make sure not to list more than four or five functions performed. This structure helps to limit too much discussion about any one job position. Further, by staying broad with the descriptions, the retail store owner is able to not reveal too much about their operational structure and strategies.

Step 5 – Organizational Chart

The organizational chart section is pretty much a visual representation of the job responsibility section. The objectives here are to show each business position within the retail store, visually. Also, this structure helps to convey the chain of command for the proposed retail store.

Organizational Chart:

The organizational chart should visually show each position within the retail store as well as whom that position reports.

Business Plan Writing Tip:

The honest truth is that most people will not read the job responsibility section. However, when individuals, such as employees, come across graphs or charts, they tend to spend a little bit of time assessing the information. From this, a well-prepared organizational chart will visually educate folks about the different positions in the retail store and the chain of command expected.

Sample:

Organizational Chart

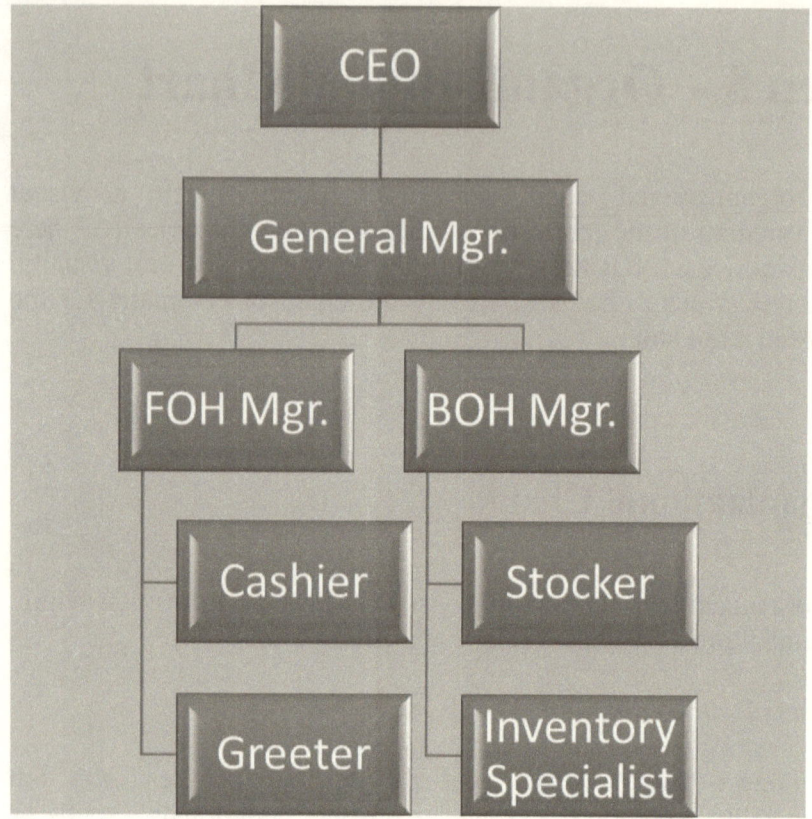

Analysis:

The chart above showed the CEO as the leader in the organization. The chain of command then moved to the store manager and assistant manager. The thorough example illustrated that both the front and back of house workers will report to the assistant manager.

Step 6 – Marketing

In the marketing section, the retail store owner has the opportunity to describe their thoughts and ideas about how the firm is going to connect with their target market. Popular forms of marketing may include social media, websites, and traditional advertising opportunities. In most instances, retail store owners are going to exploit each one of the marketing channels in order to reach their target market on multiple platforms.

Marketing Objectives and Keys to Success:

In the marketing objectives and keys to success section, I like to use a visual representation showing the company's marketing objectives, as well as identifying specific actions that the retail store owner needs to take in order to be successful.

Business Plan Writing Tip:

When writing this section, I always use a visual representation. This helps me convey, succinctly, my thoughts and ideas related to marketing and the objectives that need to be attained through the actions.

Sample:

Objectives

- Market penetration.

- Brand awareness.

- Meet customers' changing needs.

- Create marketing synergy

Keys to Success

- Selecting appropriate marketing channels.

- Continually keep customers engaged with our marketing material.

- Periodically evaluate marketing actions for optimization.

Analysis:

In the marketing objectives section, popular objectives for retail stores may include market penetration, brand building, or educating customers in relation to the products offered. As for keys to success, my preference is to focus on general actions that a retail store needs to take in order to achieve their objectives. For example, if a retail store selects the appropriate marketing channels, then the firm will achieve brand awareness.

Traditional Marketing:

Traditional marketing channels may include mailers, signage, and networking. Depending on your retail store location and theme, even your personality type, one or all of the traditional market opportunities may be exploited.

Business Plan Writing Tip:

Make sure to list and discuss all your thoughts and ideas as to the different types of traditional marketing you may implement at some point in time. Just because you may not do mailers immediately, still address this in the business plan and, in general terms, discuss your thoughts and ideas in relation to the topic.

Sample:

Traditional Marketing

Our first traditional marketing channel will include a professionally designed sign for the front of the retail store. This sign will include our retail store name, logo, and slogan. Further, prominent colors will include black, gold, and white. The objective of the signage is to let potential customers know our retail store's theme and possible products offered.

Analysis:

In most parts of the business plan, I have a strong preference for being vague and using general descriptions. This is because entrepreneurs are, and should be, paranoid about competitors finding out their strategies. However, for advertising, once a marketing campaign hits, competitors are definitely going to know the strategic thoughts and ideas behind the marketing action. From this simple fact, in the business plan, go ahead and be detailed with your traditional and other types of marketing thoughts and ideas.

Internet Marketing:

Internet marketing is any type of marketing using the internet. Common Internet marketing actions may include developing a website, blogs, Google, or Bing paid advertising, and Yelp postings.

Business Plan Writing Tip:

When writing about your Internet advertising, trying to touch on all aspects of Internet advertising that you wish to implement. For example, if you are going to have a website, make sure to talk about it, if you are going to register with Yelp or other business directories, then make sure to include this information in the business plan as well. By using this strategy, a business owner can show a broad understanding of potential internet marketing channels.

Sample:

Internet Marketing

The importance of a professionally designed website cannot be understated. To exploit this opportunity, XYZ Retail store will create and maintain a website and Yelp listing. The objective of the strategy is to effectively communicate our retail store's theme and highlight our high-end product select.

Analysis:

I identified two specific Internet advertising channels that will be exploited. The channels are a business directory, which is Yelp, and the website. Further, the objectives of Internet advertising were discussed.

Social Media Marketing:

One of the hottest and most popular forms of advertising currently is social media. Social media advertising channels may include Facebook, Instagram, and Twitter. Because of social media's popularity, new channels are continually entering the market and trending with potential customers. From this, retail store owners should not only explore and discuss using current social media channels but also review strategies to exploit new social media opportunities as well.

Business Plan Writing Tip:

A retail store owner may choose to discuss each social media advertising channel separately or go broad and outline strategic actions that may be employed in all social media channels.

Sample:

Social Media Marketing

ABC Retail store's social media advertising will include Instagram, Twitter, and Facebook. Using a three-source approach to social media will ensure our message reaches a broad audience, which will include our target market. In addition, several potential customers will receive an advertising message on multiple social media outlets. This should exceed the needed repetition of our message to a broad audience as well as our target market. The marketing message will focus on our retail store products offered and possible weekly specials.

Analysis:

In the example above, our fictitious retail store owner first introduced the different social media outlets the firm will employ. Once this was complete, the retail store owner explained, briefly, the strategy behind the social media actions. The final sentence touched on possible advertising content.

Step 7 – Financials

The financial statement section is probably the most difficult section for retail store owners to write. There are numerous reasons for this fact. First, financial statements are mostly made in Excel. Most retail store owners do not even have Excel on their computers, let alone know how to use the various functions needed to create financial statements.

Another common challenge with creating financial statements in Excel is the need to intertwine different pages. For example, when I create my financial statements, I often use one page, or tab, as an information page. The rest of the pages, located on different tabs, are tied into the information page using links and formulas. By doing this, if I change a financial figure on the information page, all of the financial statements are updated.

Financial Assumptions:

Regardless of how much time you spend on the financial statements, you will not be able to escape the simple fact that your financial statements will be wrong. I like to tell my clients that I have been writing business plans for more than ten years, and there is no way that I will know how many business plan appointments I will land tomorrow, let alone what my revenues will be in a year.

Because of this unknown, I create my financial statements based on expected revenues starting at day one. From this point, I will grow the revenues based on expected growth rates, which will be discussed in a bit.

In order to explain to the reader where the financial statement results came from, an assumption page is needed. The assumption page just tells the reader what your assumptions are for the financial statements. Common assumptions include daily sales and costs, monthly fixed costs, growth rates, tax rate, number of employees, and the cost of goods sold.

Business Plan Writing Tip:

When writing your financial assumptions page, make sure to explain any assumptions used in the financial statement calculations, starting with the top line of your income statement and ending with the bottom line of your balance sheet. For example, when I list my assumptions for clients, I usually start with the expected monthly growth estimates. From this point, I outline expected cost of goods, the advertising budget, and so on. The objective of this outline is to establish credibility for your financial statements.

Sample:

Assumptions

Our financial projections have several assumptions based on research and management's expectation of potential sales and costs.

- All financial projections are based on management and or owner(s) professional expectations of sales and expenses for the foreseeable future.

- In the first 12 months, sales should increase by approximately 5% each month. In months 13 to 24, sales growth should slow to approximately .3% per month. For years three through five, sales are expected to grow by 4.5%.

- The cost of goods or variable costs are expected to be approximately 30.21% of total sales.

- The initial advertising budget will be $7,5000. Advertising is projected to increase by approximately 1% per year. This is to ensure maximum utilization of the firm's property and equipment.

- Cost projections were calculated using a common size model. This practice is typical for financial modeling.

- The tax rate was assumed to be 20%. Fluctuation in the tax rate will have a direct impact on net profits.

- The initial funding needed is 1,500,000. An increase/decrease in amount will impact the net present value and internal rate of return.

- The starting cash balance needed is $125,000 for working capital.

- A cash account was used to balance assets with liabilities and equity.

Analysis:

In the example above, one of the first actions done was to educate and disclose the growth rate expected on a monthly basis for the first year. Further, the example went into more detail as to the reduction in the growth rate for the second year. By explaining the different growth rates, the business owner is able to show how financial sales were built.

The rest of the information just talked about various aspects of the financial statements, such as the cost of goods sold, starting budget for advertising, tax rate, initial funding, and cash that will be in the bank once the doors open for working capital. This structure lays the foundation for the business owner to justify their financial statements.

Financial Summary:

The financial summary should explain the highlights related to financial projections. These highlights include revenues and profits for the first year, expected profits for years two through five, and, when seeking funds from an investor, possibly the expected return on equity.

Business Plan Writing Tip:

When writing the financial summary section, first start off by explaining that the financial section of your business plan is based on research and observations. This disclaimer helps to set the stage for the reader's understanding that the projections are just the retail store owner's best guesses. Next, follow-up the statement with your findings from your financial analysis. These findings should include revenues for the first year, net profits, and the profit margin expected.

Sample:

Financial Summary

The financial projections are based on market research and empirical examination of the local retail store industry. For the next year, we project revenues of approximately $456,793. The estimated expense costs will be $217,330. After taxes, we estimate a net profit of $239,463. This leads to a profit margin of approximately 52.4%. As our brand continues to grow, second-year progression is anticipated to yield a net income of approximately $311,363. Within five years, net income should exceed $348,722.

Analysis:

In this example, the organization expected first-year revenues to exceed $450,000. Further, the cost involved in attaining these revenues were also shown. This helps the reader understand the potential revenue generation opportunities for the retail store and the needed cost to achieve the dollar amount noted. Other important aspects of the summary would include the net profits for years two and five.

Startup/Expansion Costs:

The startup cost section of the business plan should include the costs needed to start the retail store. If the business is already established, then this segment should outline expansion costs. If funding is being sought and the money will be used for purposes other than startup or expansion, then make sure to use this section to reflect how the money will be spent. An example of this would be if a retail store needs funds to spend on an advertising campaign, then use the section to break down the costs for the campaign implementation.

Sample:

Startup Costs	
Category	**Estimate**
Equity Investment	1,000,000.00
Loan	500,000.00
Initial Build Out	900,000
Working Capital	125,000.00
Section: Equipment	
Retail store Equipment (General)	75,000.00
FOH Inventory	35,000.00
BOH Equipment	40,000.00
Sub Total	150,000.00
Section: Operations	
Inventory	95,000.00
Supplies	150,000.00
Décor	28,000.00
Sub Total	273,000.00
Section: Office Equipment	

Office Equipment	25,000.00
Furniture	12,000.00
Sub Total	37,000.00
Section: Other	
Misc. Licenses	15,000.00
Sub Total	15,000.00
Total	**1,500,000.00**

Analysis:

When I set up my startup costs section, the first segment is always related to how much money the retail store owner has invested, funds needed from an investor, desired loan amount, if a loan is needed, initial buildout, and working capital, which are funds used for operations when the business opens.

It may be considered a little unorthodox to include funding with startup costs. However, by following this structure, the retail store owner succinctly showed funding needed and how the funds will be spent.

The rest of the sections focused on specific costs needed to start the retail store. The specific categories used were equipment, operations, office equipment, and others. In these categories, I strongly suggest that the cost estimates be inflated a bit. Say by 10 to 20 percent. Further, try to stay "general" with startup costs. This strategy is recommended simply because there is no way to know what your actual startup costs will be until your startup process has commenced.

Daily Revenues:

For my daily revenues, I always start with estimating revenues and the cost of goods for the first day of business. Revenues are the sales price multiplied by the actual number of products sold. For the cost of goods, this is considered the dollar amount that the retail store spent to make the product or service. For simplicity's sake, I always utilize a percent for the cost of goods. This helps to stay true to using averages in the financial statements.

Business Plan Writing Tip:

When designing the average daily sales segment, always use averages for everything. By embracing the concept of using averages in the financial statements, the retail store owner is acknowledging that the estimates provided in the financial statements are a best guess approximate as to what the business owner hopes to sell in the future.

Sample:

Revenue Generators							
Daily Sales	% Sales	Num.	Price	Cost	Profit	Total Rev.	Total Cost
Shirts	40%	90	35.00	14.00	21.00	3,150.00	1260
Pants	40%	90	40.00	16.00	24.00	3,600.00	1440
Access.	40%	120	15.00	6.00	9.00	1,800.00	720
					Total	11,978	4,655

Analysis:

In the first column, this is where I put the general categories for product items the retail store will sell. The first section is focused on shirts, such as women shirts, men tanks, and others. Of course, there are further differentiating factors between the clothing lines. However, for the sake of estimates, I use an average price for all shirts, pants, and so forth.

The second important item in the chart above would be "% Sales." The percent of sales are used to determine the cost of goods sold. The cost of goods sold is how much the retail store owner spends in order to buy the products. To illustrate, the cost of goods sold may be the amount of money the retail store spent on each shirt.

Labor:

Every business that has ever been started, that will ever be started, needs some type of labor involved. Even if the labor is only the retail store owner, make sure to include the labor section and the expected dollar amount to be paid on a monthly basis.

Sample:

Labor				
Employee	Number	Rate	Monthly Hours	Total Pay
Salary		n/a	n/a	4,500
Manager	1	25.00	172	4,300
Employees	18	18.00	172	55,728
			Total	60,028

Analysis:

When I create my labor template, the first line, salary, is the amount of money the retail store owner wishes to be compensated for their time and energy. Some owners may argue that they will not take a salary in the first year. However, lenders and investors, almost to the person, will want to see the owner take some kind of salary when the retail store starts. Because of this, the salary is always the first line in all of my labor financial models.

Following this line item would be managers and employees. As you can see in the example above, the structure will allow you to enter the number of managers in the average pay rate as well as the number of employees and their average pay rate. Again, we are embracing and exploiting the concept of averages.

Monthly Fixed Costs:

The monthly fixed cost segment should include any and all costs that the retail store will spend continuously, on a monthly basis. Popular fixed costs may include rent, utilities, insurance, and advertising.

Sample:

Monthly Fixed Costs	
Monthly Costs	**Monthly Total**
Rent	15,000
Utilities	1,580
Office Expenses	780
Insurance	400
Accounting/legal	250
Advertising	7500
Other	650
Monthly Total	26,160

Analysis:

Fixed costs are definitely a misnomer. Just because we call them "fixed costs" does not mean the costs will not change on a monthly basis. The fixed costs title is more focused on the actual items being paid as compared to the same dollar amount paid each month.

When constructing the fixed costs segment, there are a couple of different theories that may be applied to the construction of the segment. First, some retail store owners prefer to leave fixed costs as the same dollar amount throughout the year and then add a growth estimate for the next year.

Other owners prefer to use a percentage of sales approach. In this approach, costs that change on a monthly basis, such as utilities, office expenses, and "other," would be based on a percent of sales technique. In this technique, each variable line item would be divided by sales. For subsequent months fixed costs, the line items would be calculated by multiplying the percent found in the first month for the line item by sales in the following months. This technique is known as common sizing.

Growth Rates:

Growth rates are the percentages used to increase a line item due to growth or inflation. Not surprisingly, different sections of the financial estimates will grow at different paces. From this, the need for a section related to growth rates is needed.

Sample:

Growth Rates	
Growth Rate Sales 2 & 3	3.50%
Growth Rate Sales 4 & 5	1.50%
Growth Rate Cost of Goods	1.50%
Growth Rate Salary	1.50%

Growth Rate Labor	3.00%
Growth Advertising	1.00%
Growth Office	1.00%
Growth Utility	1.00%
Growth Legal	1.00%
Growth Insurance	1.00%
Growth Other	1.00%

Analysis:

My preference for the growth rates is to show different growth rates for each category. Labor is bound to grow at a different pace than say business insurance. This structure allows for the needed adjustments.

Misc. Information:

The miscellaneous information section is pretty much used as a catchall for adjusting various line items in the financial statements. This segment may include the tax rate, cost of capital for the retail store, franchise royalty payments, etc.

Sample:

Misc. Information	
Tax Rate	20%
Cost of Capital	10%

Analysis:

In this section, I usually only include the tax rate and cost of capital. For most instances, the cost of capital is not really needed. However, the tax rate is essential for determining estimated taxes that the retail store will pay on a monthly and annual basis.

Loan Payment Calculation:

When obtaining a loan, banks often prefer to calculate the loan information using their proprietary software. However, the business owner should still use the Excel function for calculating payments and include the information in their financial statements. An important concept to keep in mind for the income statement is to make sure they subtract interest paid instead of the full monthly payment for the loan. Not only is this standard procedure for accounting, but it also helps to show increased revenues.

Sample:

Loan Information	
Loan Amount	(500,000.00)
Interest Rate	7%
Term	25
Payment	$3,533.90

Analysis:

In this example above, a loan is expected to be taken out for $500,000. The interest rate is expected to be 7% with a term of 25 years. As a result, the retail store owner will be expected to pay $3,533.90 on a monthly basis. As noted above, for the profit and loss statement as well as the income statement, the monthly interest payment is the portion used. To find the interest portion, the amortization schedule is needed.

Profit and Loss for 12 Months:

The profit and loss statement shows the revenues, costs, taxes, and profits for your retail store. My preference is to break up the 12-month profit and loss statement into monthly segments and then total each month quarterly. By doing this, the retail store owner is able to see the monthly growth projections, as well as the costs aligned with the projected revenues.

Business Plan Writing Tip:

When creating your 12-month profit and loss statement, make sure to always use Excel or some other spreadsheet. This will allow you to do calculations easily and duplicate your work month over month.

When creating your profit and loss statement, make sure to always start with your revenues and then align the cost of goods and other fixed costs with your monthly sales. By following this process, the retail store owner is able to see how much money the retail store can make and what costs are involved with the process.

Sample:

Pro Forma Income Statement Year 1 Quarter 1				
	Month 1	**Month 2**	**Month 3**	**Quarter 1**
Revenues	192,941	198,729	204,691	596,361
COGS	57,145	58,859	60,625	176,629
Gross Profit	135,796	139,870	144,066	419,732
Expenses				
Salary	4,500	4,500	4,500	13,500
Labor	60,028	60,028	60,028	180,084
Advertising	7,500	7,500	7,500	22,500
Office Expen.	780	803	828	2,411

Rent	15,000	15,000	15,000	45,000
Utilities	1,580	1,627	1,676	4,884
Legal / Account	250	250	250	750
Insurance	400	400	400	1,200
Depreciation	11,667	11,667	11,667	35,000
Other	650	650	650	1,950
Total Expenses	102,355	102,425	102,498	307,279
EBIT	33,441	37,445	41,568	112,454
Interest Expense	2,917	2,913	2,909	8,739
EBT	30,525	34,532	38,658	103,715
Taxes	6,105	6,906	7,732	20,743
Net Income	24,420	27,625	30,927	82,972

Pro Forma Income Statement - Common Size				
Income Statement	**Month 1**	**Month 2**	**Month 3**	**Quarter 1**
Sales Growth	**3.00%**	**3.00%**	**3.00%**	**6.09%**
Revenues	100.00%	100.00%	100.00%	100.00%
Costs of goods Sold	29.62%	29.62%	29.62%	29.62%
Gross Profit	70.38%	70.38%	70.38%	70.38%
Expenses				
Salary	2.33%	2.26%	2.20%	2.20%
Labor	31.11%	31.11%	31.11%	31.11%

Advertising	3.89%	3.89%	3.89%	3.89%
Office Expenses	0.40%	0.40%	0.40%	0.40%
Rent	7.77%	7.77%	7.77%	7.77%
Utilities	0.82%	0.82%	0.82%	0.82%
Legal / Accounting	0.13%	0.13%	0.13%	0.13%
Insurance	0.21%	0.21%	0.21%	0.21%
Depreciation	6.05%	6.05%	6.05%	6.05%
Other	0.34%	0.34%	0.34%	0.34%
Total Expenses	53.05%	51.54%	50.07%	51.53%
EBIT	17.33%	18.84%	20.31%	18.86%
Interest Expense	1.51%	1.47%	1.42%	1.47%
Earnings before taxes	15.82%	17.38%	18.89%	17.39%
Taxes	3.16%	3.48%	3.78%	3.48%
Net Income	12.66%	13.90%	15.11%	13.91%

Analysis:

In this example, first, start with the revenues that are projected for the month. In order to give first-month revenues, I always go back to my expected daily sales. Using daily sales, I will then multiply the daily sales by 30 and the cost of goods by 30. This will give me my first-month sales and the cost of goods.

Next, identify the fixed costs aligned with the monthly sales and deduct them from the gross profits, which is just revenue subtracted by the cost of goods sold. Once this is complete, just subtract any interest expenses and taxes. This leaves the retail store's net income.

To determine the second-month profit and loss, first, start by multiplying the revenues by an expected monthly growth rate. Next, for costs that increase on a monthly basis, based on sales, use the common size financial document. For example, in the example above, the office expense was .4% of sales. From this, we would multiply .4% by the new revenues for the next 12-months to determine the expected office supplies costs. This practice would be used for labor, office expenses, and utilities, as well. Keep in mind, for some costs, such as rent, advertising, insurance, and salary; these costs will remain the same, usually, for the first 12-months.

Income Statement:

The income statement is simply the total of your 12 months profit and loss statements. In other words, the income statement shows the total revenues and costs for the first 12-months. Once this is complete, most income statements will then project revenues, costs, and profits for the next four years, giving the retail store owner a five-year income statement projection to review.

Business Plan Writing Tip:

When creating your income statement, my preference is to first construct a table showing quarterly profit and losses, as shown below. Next, total the quarterly profits and losses into an annual column. With this complete, create a table using the annual revenues, costs and include columns for years two through five. The next step is to utilize our growth projections, as noted earlier, and multiply each line item by the associated growth projection. This will result in a five-year income statement, as shown below.

Sample:

Pro Forma Income Statement Annual Summary				
Quarter 1	Quarter 2	Quarter 3	Quarter 4	Annual

Revenues	596,361	651,660	712,087	778,116	2,738,224
COGS	176,629	193,007	210,904	230,461	811,001
Gross Profit	419,732	458,653	501,182	547,655	1,927,223
	-	-	-	-	-
Expenses					
Salary	13,500	13,500	13,500	13,500	54,000
Labor	180,084	180,084	180,084	180,084	720,336
Advertising	22,500	22,500	22,500	22,500	90,000
Office Expen.	2,411	2,610	2,852	3,116	10,988
Rent	45,000	45,000	45,000	45,000	180,000
Utilities	4,884	5,286	5,776	6,312	22,258
Legal / Account	750	750	750	750	3,000
Insurance	1,200	1,200	1,200	1,200	4,800
Deprec.	35,000	35,000	35,000	35,000	140,000
Other	1,950	1,950	1,950	1,950	7,800
Total Expenses	307,279	307,880	308,612	309,412	1,233,182
	-	-	-	-	-
EBIT	112,454	150,773	192,570	238,243	694,041
Interest Expense	8,739	8,706	8,673	8,639	34,758
EBT	103,715	142,067	183,897	229,604	659,283
Taxes	20,743	28,413	36,779	45,921	131,857
Net Income	82,972	113,653	147,118	183,684	527,426

Pro Forma Income Statement - Base					
	Year 1	Year 2	Year 3	Year 4	Year 5
Revenues	2,738,224	3,266,320	3,380,641	3,431,351	3,482,821
COGS	811,001	967,412	981,923	996,652	1,011,601
Gross Profit	1,927,223	2,298,908	2,398,718	2,434,699	2,471,220
Expenses					
Salary	54,000	54,810	55,632	56,467	57,314
Labor	720,336	741,946	764,204	787,131	810,745
Advertis.	90,000	90,900	91,809	92,727	93,654
Office Expenses	10,988	13,195	13,327	13,460	13,595
Rent	180,000	180,000	180,000	180,000	180,000
Utilities	22,258	26,729	26,996	27,266	27,538
Legal / Accoun	3,000	3,030	3,060	3,091	3,122
Insurance	4,800	4,848	4,896	4,945	4,995
Deprec.	140,000	237,500	168,150	124,020	117,090
Other	7,800	7,878	7,957	8,036	8,117
Total Expenses	1,233,182	1,360,836	1,316,032	1,297,143	1,316,169
EBIT	694,041	938,073	1,082,686	1,137,556	1,155,050
Interest Expense	34,758	34,205	33,612	32,976	32,294
Earnings before taxes	659,283	903,868	1,049,074	1,104,580	1,122,756
Taxes	131,857	180,774	209,815	220,916	224,551
Net Income	527,426	723,094	839,260	883,664	898,205

Analysis:

I started with the quarterly expected profit and loss projections that we calculated in the 12-month profit and loss section. Next, I added together the quarterly projections to come up with the first-year income statement projection. Once this was completed, I used the growth rates discussed in the growth rate section to project the next four years' profit and losses in the income statement.

Balance Sheet:

The balance sheet is, for the most part, not absolutely needed in the business plan. This is because the projections for the balance sheet will almost always be significantly off as compared to actual results. However, for the diehard entrepreneurs looking to cover all aspects of their financial expectations, presented below is a sample balance sheet.

Business Plan Writing Tip:

When discussing the balance sheet, make sure to explicitly state that the projections for the financial statement may change based on sales, operations, and other business needs. I like to put the statement before the balance sheet because of the significant fluctuation between projected returns and the actual results in the balance sheet.

When discussing the balance sheet, make sure to highlight the cash position and retained earnings. The cash position is important because this will show the reader that you, as the owner, expect to have enough liquid assets to operate the retail store for the short and long term. As for the retained earnings, this section is where your net profit, minus dividends paid, ties into your balance sheet.

If your retained earnings grow at the same pace as your net profits, then this shows that your retail store reinvests most of the profits earned. However, if the segment grows at a significantly slower pace as compared to your net income, then investors and bankers may ascertain that a significant amount of your net profits are being paid out to the founder as dividends or other owners.

Sample:

Balance Sheet - Pro Forma					
Assets	**Year 1**	**Year 2**	**Year 3**	**Year 4**	**Year 5**
Cash	867,202	1,821,416	2,821,905	3,822,085	4,830,119
Accts Receiv.	-	-	-	-	-
Inventories	67,583	80,618	81,827	83,054	84,300
Total Curr. Assets	934,785	1,902,034	2,903,732	3,905,139	4,914,419
PP&E	1,360,000	1,360,000	1,360,000	1,360,000	1,360,000
Less Deprec.	140,000	377,500	545,650	669,670	786,760
Net PP&E	1,220,000	982,500	814,350	690,330	573,240
Total Assets	2,154,785	2,884,534	3,718,082	4,595,469	5,487,659

Balance Sheet - Pro Forma					
Liabilities	**Year 1**	**Year 2**	**Year 3**	**Year 4**	**Year 5**
Accounts Pay	67,583	80,618	81,827	83,054	84,300
Notes Payable	2,896	2,850	2,801	2,748	2,691
Accruals	64,528	66,396	68,320	70,300	72,338
Total Current Liab.	135,008	149,864	152,948	156,102	159,329
Loans	492,351	484,149	475,354	465,923	456,681
Total Liabilities	627,359	634,013	628,302	622,025	616,010

Common Stock	1,000,000	1,000,000	1,000,000	1,000,000	1,000,000
Retained Earnings	527,426	1,250,521	2,089,780	2,973,444	3,871,649
Total Com. Equity	1,527,426	2,250,521	3,089,780	3,973,444	4,871,649
Total Liab & Equity	2,154,785	2,884,534	3,718,082	4,595,469	5,487,659

Analysis:

In the example above, the retail store owner can see that the retained earnings section of the balance sheet grows significantly year-over-year. This shows that the owner intends to reinvest a significant portion of their net profits back into the retail store. By doing this, the retail store owner increases the likelihood of success in the business.

Further, the example above showed the cash position grown significantly over a five-year time span. This also helps the retail store owner show that they fully expect enough liquidity to support operations for the short and long term.

Financial Ratios:

Financial ratios utilize a retail store's financial projections to show how efficient or profitable and organization will be based on the owner's best estimate. Common financial ratios include:
- Return on equity
- Return on assets
- Current ratio
- Profit margin

Return on Equity - Almost all investors are crazy about return on equity. This is because the return on equity indicates to investors how much the retail store profited in relation to equity invested. As shown below, the calculation for return on equity is net income divided by total equity. Investors want to see this ratio as high as possible and climbing over time. This is because either a retail store is increasing its net income by using the same amount of equity invested or the firm is using less equity to generate the same amount of money.

Formula:

$$ROE = Net\ Income\ /\ Total\ Equity$$

Return on Assets - In keeping with the profitability thing, the return on assets allows investors to assess how profitable our target organization is as compared to the total assets utilized by the organization. With this ratio, investors prefer to see a relatively high return on assets. This indicates that the organization is generating net profits from assets as a whole.

Formula:

$$ROA = Net\ Income\ /\ Total\ Assets$$

Current Ratio - One of the most popular financial ratios is the current ratio. The current ratio measures the amount of cash inflow (money coming into the retail store) over the last 12-months with the amount of cash outflow (bills that needed to be paid by the retail store). From this measurement, we can determine whether the retail store had enough money coming in to cover funds going out.

Formula:

$$Current\ Ratio = Current\ Assets\ /\ Current\ Liabilities$$

In the above formula, we can see that if a retail store has more current assets than current liabilities, the answer will always be greater than one. However, if a retail store has more current liabilities as compared to current assets, then the answer is going to be less than one.

Profit Margin - My personal favorite financial ratio is the profit margin. The profit margin ratio compares a retail store's net income, or profits, with their revenues. Again, the higher this ratio, the better for investors. A distressing trend to be cognizant of, as an investor, is when the profit margin increases when revenues fall. This happens because management has taken it upon themselves to significantly cut costs within the retail store. Unfortunately, this type of action is not sustainable. Further, cost-cutting often leads to long-term revenue decline.

Formula:

Profit Margin = Net Income / Total Revenues

Business Plan Writing Tip:

When writing the financial ratio section of the business plan, don't just provide the ratios, make sure to explain what the ratios actually mean. By doing this, the entrepreneur adds credibility to the calculations. Also, this will help show the importance of the ratios selected.

Sample:

Financial Ratios					
	Year 1	Year 2	Year 3	Year 4	Year 5
Return on Equity	34.53%	32.13%	27.16%	22.24%	18.44%
Return on Asset	24.48%	25.07%	22.57%	19.23%	16.37%
Current Ratio	6.92	12.69	18.99	25.02	30.84
Profit	19.26%	22.14%	24.83%	25.75%	25.79%

Margin						
Net Present Value	9,050,885					
IRR	83.40%					

Analysis:

In the sample above, the business owner expected to provide investors with a return on equity in the first year of 34.5%. As the organization grows, the return on equity is expected to decrease. Usually, this situation happens when the business owner continually reinvests their net profits. In other words, the business owner intends to utilize equity for growth opportunities as compared to taking on debt.

For the return on assets, the business owner in the scenario anticipates a 24.4% return on assets for the first year. This is anticipated to decline to 16.3% in year five. The reduction in return on assets may be partly due to holding a significant amount of cash. From the perspective of an investor, this may be of a minor concern because the excessive cash holding may be preferable than taking on additional risk for a startup retail store.

As for the current ratio, this shows that the business intends to have a significant cash position in the first year and grow this position for the next several years. As a result, the business owner will have more than enough current assets to pay for their current liabilities.

As for the profit margin, this also is projected to increase. Specifically, the profit margin is anticipated to grow from 19.26% in year 1 to 25.79% in year 5. This indicates that the business owner expects revenues to increase at a faster pace than the cost of goods and fixed costs.

Step 8 – Funding Request

The funding request section should include four important components, which are potential funding sources, funding terms, use of funds, and fund repayment.

Sample:

Funding Request

To start operations, funding of $1,500,000 in debt or equity from a bank or investor is required. Debt funding is expected to have a term of 15 to 20 years with an interest rate between 8% to 10%. Principle and interest payments will be made monthly, using profits from the business. For investors, a negotiated percentage of ownership in the retail store will be offered. In addition, after the second year of profitability, investors will be compensated through semi-annually dividend payments from business cash flows.

Received funds will be used as follows:

Startup Costs	
Category	**Estimate**
Equity Investment	1,000,000.00
Loan	500,000.00
Initial Build Out	900,000
Working Capital	125,000.00
Section: Equipment	
Retail store Equipment (General)	75,000.00
FOH Equipment	35,000.00
BOH Equipment	40,000.00
Sub Total	150,000.00

Section: Operations	
Inventory	95,000.00
Supplies	150,000.00
Décor	28,000.00
Sub Total	273,000.00
Section: Office Equipment	
Office Equipment	25,000.00
Furniture	12,000.00
Sub Total	37,000.00
Section: Other	
Misc. Licenses	15,000.00
Sub Total	15,000.00
Total	**1,500,000.00**

Potential Funding Sources:

The potential funding source, or sources, are all of the channels that the retail store owner may use to obtain funding for their organization. Popular funding sources include lending institutions, such as banks, private investors, and grants. Most recently, crowdfunding has become a popular source of financing, as well.

Business Plan Writing Tip:

Make sure to discuss every source that may be considered for funding. Common sources include investors and lending institutions, such as banks or credit unions. However, other funding sources are available, as well. These may include grants or crowdfunding opportunities.

Sample:

To start operations, funding of $1,500,000 in debt or equity from a bank or investor is required.

Analysis:

As shown in the example above, for this retail store owner, lending sources are limited to investors and lending institutions. If the owner decided to explore grants or crowdfunding opportunities, then the business plan should be updated to reflect these aspirations.

Funding Terms:

Funding terms are the range of terms that the retail store owner will entertain. Funding terms may include a range of interest rates that would be acceptable to the owner for a loan. As for investors, terms with this party is a little bit more complicated. From this, just stating that an equity position is negotiable often will suffice.

Business Plan Writing Tip:

In the funding term section, make sure to tell the potential lender or investor your expectations or parameters for funding. These parameters should include a dollar amount for the loan or equity investment, length of time for loan, expected interest rate, or offer for a percentage of the retail store to potential investors.

Sample:

Debt funding is expected to have a term of 15 to 20 years with an interest rate between 8% to 10%.

And

For investors, a negotiated percentage of ownership in the retail store will be offered.

Analysis:

The dollar amount expected, or need is $1.5 million. For this particular segment, a specific dollar amount is highly recommended. However, in certain situations, a range of funding may be acceptable. Just make sure to explain why the range of funds is needed.

The second part is related to the term expected for the loan, which is between 15 and 20 years. For most other instances of the business funding request, ranges are more than acceptable; they are actually recommended to be honest.

Use of Funds:

The use of funds section is where the retail store owner shows the investor or lender where their money will be spent. A common use of funds includes working capital, which is money needed for general operations, the buildout of a location, if you need to rent an office space or retail space, and purchasing inventory.

Business Plan Writing Tip:

When I write a use of funds section, I always put the information in a spreadsheet and show a total at the bottom. Further, when categorizing the use of funds, try to use broad categories, such as office equipment, storage equipment, etc. By staying general with the categories, this allows the retail store owner to use the funds as needed, but within the general budget.

Sample:

Startup Costs	
Category	Estimate
Equity Investment	1,000,000.00
Loan	500,000.00

Initial Build Out	900,000
Working Capital	125,000.00
Section: Equipment	
Retail store Equipment (General)	75,000.00
FOH Equipment	35,000.00
BOH Equipment	40,000.00
Sub Total	150,000.00
Section: Operations	
Inventory	95,000.00
Supplies	150,000.00
Décor	28,000.00
Sub Total	273,000.00
Section: Office Equipment	
Office Equipment	25,000.00
Furniture	12,000.00
Sub Total	37,000.00
Section: Other	
Misc. Licenses	15,000.00
Sub Total	15,000.00
Total	**1,500,000.00**

Analysis:

In the example provided, my use of funds section is broken into segments to help with budgeting purposes. The segment utilized were equipment, operations, and office equipment. Further, in the structure provided, I also offer some totals for each segment. Not only does this show a well-thought-out startup funding structure, but this also helps the investor or loan officer ascertain whether some of the budgetary segments are in line with expectations.

Fund Repayment:

The fund repayment section will tell the investor or loan officer/underwriter how the loan or equity investment will be rewarded. For the most part, dividends and loan payments will be paid from profits in the retail store. This may seem like common sense to you and me. However, surprisingly enough, some people actually pay funds from other businesses or even from retirement accounts. By explaining how the funds will be repaid, the investor or loan officer will have a full picture of how their investment will be compensated.

Business Plan Writing Tip:

When writing this section, I prefer to have the fund repayment information addressed in the final paragraph. This allows the investing parties to understand the totality of the funding situation before being introduced to the repayment segment.

Sample:

Principle and interest payments will be made monthly, using profits from the business. For investors, a negotiated percentage of ownership in the retail store will be offered. In addition, after the second year of profitability, investors will be compensated through semi-annually dividend payments from business cash flows.

Analysis:

In the example provided, funds used to repay vested parties are clearly stated in the funding request. Further, principal and interest payments come from profits in the retail store on a monthly basis. As for investors, their compensation will also come from cash flow in the retail store, but only after the second-year of profitability.

Step 9 – Executive Summary

The executive summary is the first section that a business owner should present to the interested party. When I write my executive summaries, they are always an abbreviated version of the business plan. By doing this, essentially, a business owner has two documents. The first document may be considered an executive summary. This will briefly explain, in broad terms, what the retail store is about, the products offered, differentiated items provided, financial outlook, and funds needed to start operations or grow the retail store.

Retail Store and Product:

The retail store and product section should briefly summarize the retail store and inventory items being offered.

Business Plan Writing Tip:

When I write this section, I will always copy and paste my retail store summary and product description under the heading for the executive summary. Next, I literally just start deleting lines to reduce the content to approximately a paragraph.

For the second paragraph, I will then summarize the rest of the retail store description section of the business plan, such as competitive advantage, hours of operation, number of employees, and any other critical pieces of information that I to show upfront about the retail store.

Sample:

XYZ Retail store is a limited liability retail store located in Orlando, Florida. Our retail store's main product line will be clothing. To complement our clothing lines, we will also offer jewelry, shoes, hats, and gloves. Our retail store specializes in high-end clothing in a welcoming ambiance.

Our retail store uses the best value pricing model to ensure a competitive price is offered to our customers. Our hours of operation are from 6:00 AM to 3 PM, seven days a week. Our staff size is 12, including the owner. An important key to success in sustaining our business is to continually engage our target market through innovative advertising messages.

Analysis:

In the first paragraph, the location of the establishment, inventory items, and differentiating factors are almost always discussed. This immediately shows the type of retail store and how it is different from other retail stores in the area.

As for the second paragraph, this is always a summary of the rest of the information in the retail store description. I like to include the hours of operation, staff size, and how the retail store will sustain operations in the long term.

Target Market:

The target market, as noted earlier in the book, is a demographic or group of individuals that may frequently visit our retail store.

Business Plan Writing Tip:

For this section, I just simply note the target market and eliminate any additional information as to why the selection was made.

Sample:

Our primary target market will be young executive-level works, specifically females between the ages of 25 to 35.

Analysis:

The sample tells shows the type of worker, age bracket, and gender of our target market and nothing more.

Financial Highlights:

The financial highlights section of the executive summary should stay focused on how the retail store will perform financially over the next 12-months. Because of this limited focus, popular inclusions in the financial highlight summary section would be related to first-year annual profits, expenses aligned with these prophets, and net profits expected.

Business Plan Writing Tip:

I like to keep this section to approximately four lines. Further, I always first introduce the revenues and then the cost aligned with the revenues. With this done, I finished the paragraph with net profits and the profit margin ratio. The succinct financial summary shows investors or loan officers the retail store's potential profits in short order.

Sample:

The financial projections are based on market research and empirical examination of the local retail store industry. For the next year, we project revenues of approximately $456,793. The estimated expense costs will be $217,330. After taxes, we estimate a net profit of $239,463. This leads to a profit margin of approximately 52.4%.

Analysis:

The summarized version of the financial summary is definitely short and sweet. The most important aspects of the financial statements are included in the short paragraph. Further, the structure of the financial summary almost tells a story. First, it starts with revenues, then shows the cost involved with the revenues. Once the costs are deducted, then the profits are shown. Finally, a real quick ratio was presented, as well.

Funding:

Differing from the other sections in the executive summary, the funding section should be almost identical to the funding section in the business plan, with the exception of the cost breakdown. Not surprisingly, investors want to know how much money the retail store needs and how they will be repaid. There is no skimping on details here.

Business Plan Writing Tip:

The section should be written in terms similar to, or identical to, the funding section of the business plan, as noted above.

Sample:

To start operations, funding of $1,500,000 in debt or equity from a bank or investor is required. Debt funding is expected to have a term of 15 to 20 years with an interest rate between 8% to 10%. Principle and interest payments will be made monthly, using profits from the retail store. For investors, a negotiated percentage of ownership in the retail store will be offered. In addition, after the second year of profitability, investors will be compensated through semi-annually dividend payments from business cash flows.

Analysis:

Not much need for analysis. Just copy and paste and ignore the startup cost. You are now ready to go.

Step 10 – Appendix

The appendix section is used for charts, graphs, and other documents that support the business plan.

Resumes:

For almost all business plans, I will include the retail store owner's resume in the appendix section. The resume helps to support experiences noted in the management and organization section of the business plan.

Business Plan Writing Tip:

When including a resume in a business plan, stay away from the pictures and fancy fonts. Usually, the reader is more interested in understanding the retail store owners' experiences and education related to the proposed business.

Sample:

Paul Borosky

XXX Rachelle Dr. Apt XXX - Sanford, FL. 32771 - (321) 948-****–
Paulb@Qualitybusinessplan.com

Professional Experience

Quality Business Plan
Plan Writing
Sanford, Fl. / Online

Business Consulting – Business

* Prepared pro forma financial
statements.

October 2010 - Present   * Research various industries for trends, revenues, and growth projections.
      * Calculate various financial ratios such as Return on Equity and Current Ratio.
      * Write business plans for current and prospective businesses.

XXX High school   **Entrepreneurship / Microsoft Office / Computer Programming Instructor**
Durham, NC.   * Prepare lesson plans for Excel, Word, Visual Basic, and other classes.
August, 2014 – October, 2016   * Assign and grade various assignments.
      * Provide in-depth student feedback in residential settings.
      * Assist students through numerous stages of learning.

XXX College   **Resident and Online Adjunct Finance / Entrepreneurship Instructor**
Ocala, Fl.   * Prepare lesson plans for residential class.
June, 2013 – December 2016   * Assign and grade various finance assignments.
      * Provide in-depth student feedback in residential and online settings.
      * Assist students through numerous stages of learning.
      * Subject Matter Expert – Created and Designed college level finance classes.

Walt Disney World Resorts   **Quick Service Food -**
Supervisor
Orlando, Fl.   * Prepared guest meals in fast pace environment.
April, 2011-Jan, 2013   * Display exceptional customer service to guest.
      * Daily practice Disney's leader basics.
      * Lead other cast members by example and instruction.

Education

Northcentral University	DBA, Management – Doctoral Candidate Ongoing
Webster University	Finance – 21 Master level credit hours 2011
Webster University (MBA)	Masters in Business Administration 2010
Barry University	Bachelors in Professional Studies with specialization in Administration 2009
Seminole State College	AA Degree 2002

Training and Skills

Blackboard Learning System	Rasmussen College 2016
Microsoft PowerPoint Certified	Certiport 2016
Microsoft Excel Certified	Certiport 2016
Microsoft Word Certified	Certiport 2015
Canvas Learning System	Voyager High School 2015
NC Department of Education License	Temporary Professional Educator's 2014
Angel Learning System	Rasmussen College 2013
Fl. Department of Education Business (grades 6-12)	Statement of Status of Eligibility – 2013
Online Faculty Training	Rasmussen College 2013
Salesforce	Training for Salesforce software 2013

Analysis:

In this example, the proposed retail store owner starts off by highlighting the professional experiences. In some cases, educational experiences may come first. The decision really depends on where the most experience lies. If the owner has significant work experience, then go with professional experiences first. However, if education better supports the retail store concept, then, by all means, rearrange your resume to lead off with education. A final analysis note would be that there is no variation in colors, fancy fonts, or other tactics to spruce up the resume design. Always keep in mind, the star of the show is a retail store and not the owner.

Summary

In summary, the retail store business plan writing process is definitely long, tedious, and detailed, to say the least. However, by following the discussed business plan writing process in this book AND by using the sample and template provided, you now have the tools and training to complete your very own retail store business plan!

Best of luck with your endeavor!

Retail Store Business Plan Sample

Executive Summary

Retail store Summary: XYZ Retail store is a limited liability retail store located in Orlando, Florida. Our retail store's main product line will be clothing. To complement our clothing lines, we will also offer jewelry, shoes, hats, and gloves. Our retail store specializes in high-end clothing in a welcoming ambiance.

Our retail store uses the best value pricing model to ensure a competitive price is offered to our customers. Our hours of operation are from 6:00 AM to 3 PM, seven days a week. Our staff size is 12, including the owner. An important key to success in sustaining our business is to continually engage our target market through innovative advertising messages.

Target Market: Our primary target market will be young executive-level works, specifically females between the ages of 25 to 35.

Financial Highlights: The financial projections are based on market research and empirical examination of the local retail store industry. For the next year, we project revenues of approximately $456,793. The estimated expense costs will be $217,330. After taxes, we estimate a net profit of $239,463. This leads to a profit margin of approximately 52.4%.

Funding Request: To start operations, funding of $1,500,000 in debt or equity from a bank or investor is required. Debt funding is expected to have a term of 15 to 20 years with an interest rate between 8% to 10%. Principle and interest payments will be made monthly, using profits from the retail store. For investors, a negotiated percentage of ownership in the retail store will be offered. Also, after the second year of profitability, investors will be compensated through semi-annually dividend payments from business cash flows.

Retail store Description

Retail store Summary

ABC Retail store will be a limited liability corporation located at 123 Broadway St. in Orlando, FL. Our business owner(s) will be John Smith. Our retail store's main product line will be clothing. To complement our clothing lines, we will also offer jewelry, shoes, hats, and gloves. Our hours of operation will be from 8 AM To 8:30 PM, seven days a week.

Competitive Advantages

ABC company will have specific competitive advantages once our firm starts operations. First, our retail store will sell high-quality, name-branded products from companies that have pledged to embrace eco-friendly practices. No other retail store in the area has committed to this business model. Further, our firm will embrace the "full-attire" concept in our product offerings. For our full-attire concept, we will employ knowledgeable associates that are able to help customers match clothing with accessories to create unique looks based on our customer's taste.

Products Description

Shirts
Our shirts product lines may include Polo, Under Armour, Nike, and other named brand companies dedicated to offering high-quality shirt products and supports corporate social responsibility.

Pants:
The pants product line will focus on brand names like Levi's, St. John, and Ralph Lauren. As for type, we will carry straight leg, Ultraflex, and boot cut.

Accessories:
To round out any outfit, we will carry a wide selection of sunglasses, jewelry, shoes, and other items that may be trending or in high demand for customers.

For a full product selection, please review Appendix A.

Pricing Strategy

Our pricing structure will be focused on the best value strategy. For this strategy, our management team will continually research the prices of clothing lines offered by local retail store competitors in the area. From this research, we will create base inventory item prices using the averages of competitors in the area. Next, our organization will make product item price adjustments based on the quality of the clothing line, the ambiance of the competitors' establishment, and overall clothing line selection as compared to ours. The end objective is to have all of our products prices competitively priced using the best value strategic model.

Business Models

Operations:
Our operational structure will seek to achieve a high-end retail store's breadth of product selections while offering access to knowledgeable attendants. As a customer approaches our retail store, they will be met with advertising decals on the door and smiling attendants at the entrance. This will allow visitors to feel at home while they shop for their clothing needs. At the counter, our visitors will be offered complimentary products and accessories to their purchases. This will ensure a complete wardrobe makeover after each visit.

Hours of Operations:
Our hours of operations business model will be structured to ensure our retail store customers' needs are met at a convenient time. From this, our organization will be open from 8 AM to 8:30 PM, seven days a week.

Location

As previously stated, our location will be in the Orlando, Florida, area. The proposed location size will be about 4,500 square feet. Approximately three-quarters of the area will be dedicated to the shopping space for customers. The rest of the area will be devoted to the back of the house operations like storage, office space, and packaging.

As for competition, this area has few other high-end clothing retail stores within a several miles radius. This will enable us to capture a significant portion of the casual retail market in the area.

Future Plans

Within the next 24 months, our firm will open new locations in the Orlando / Central Florida area. The new sites and timeframe will be based on funding, leadership availability, and other factors. Further, our management team will introduce new product items within the next 12 months. These items will be selected based on customer demand, how well the items complement our current offering and the availability of the products.

Business Objectives and Timeline

1 - 3 Months
- o   Obtain investor funding.
- o   Identify the facility and negotiate a rental agreement.
- o   Engage in buildout activities.
- o   Open for business.

3 – 6 Months
- o   Start an advertising campaign.
- o   Evaluate marketing strategy and implement it.
- o   Evaluate business models.

6 – 12 Months
- o   Optimize marketing strategies.
- o   Optimize business models.
- o   Examine external environment for market opportunities.

Mission Statement

"Our retail store's mission is to provide the best name brand selections in a friendly atmosphere and clean environment."

Vision Statement

"Deliver world-class wardrobe changes using named brand products on a global level."

Value Statement

- o Honesty.
- o Fair prices.
- o Named brand clothing.
- o Technical innovations

Keys to Success

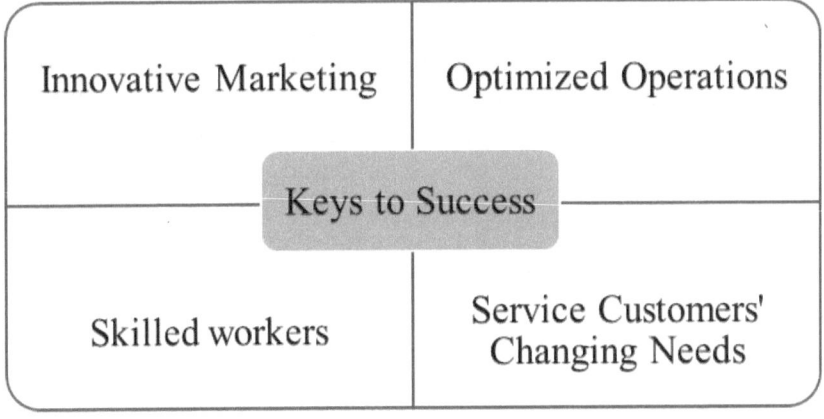

Target Market

Primary Target Market

Our primary target market will be young, blue-collar works. Specifically, females between the ages of 25 to 35. This demographic was selected because of their propensity to enjoy named brand clothing while shopping in a comfortable environment.

Secondary Target Market

As for the secondary target market, this will be medical professionals working at the hospital across the street or in medical facilities surrounding the hospital. This demographic was selected due to its proximity to our retail store.

Target Market Growth

Based on research from website XYZ, the current executive-level workforce in ABC City is 25,000 people. The U.S. Census Bureau has noted that the city's population increased by 1.3% annually over the last five years. Based on this factor, our retail store owner expects a similar growth rate for the next five years. From this, the target market formulation will be 25,325 within the next 12 months. In two years, our target market population will expand to 25,655 people.

Market Analysis

Industry Overview

Family clothing stores cater to men, women, and children through a wide array of product offerings like shirts, pants, and trending accessories. This industry is expected to exceed $110 billion in sales next year. To support further growth, industry experts project between a 1% to 1.3% growth rate.

Industry Statistics

- Industry experts predict that athletic wear will outpace other product lines by over 50% for the next several years.
- Women's clothing sales are projected to encapsulate 50% of all clothing items sold.
- Brick-and-mortar retail establishments have been entering the online retail space to complement their services at a faster pace than previous years.
- Customers' tastes tend to change faster with apparel than with other mature industries.

Threats, Trends, and Opportunities

An important threat to the industry would be related to the overall economy. Currently, job growth and employment are at all-time-highs. From this, people have enough discretionary funds to afford high-end apparel. Unfortunately, in the event of an economic recession, as discretionary funds for people decrease, profits for the retail store industry may show a correlated effect.

As for an opportunity, high-end retail shoppers are increasing selecting "mom and pop" retail stores over chain retail locations due to better service and appealing product selections. This allows for startup retail stores to enter the market place and gain a loyal following. Finally, trends in the retail store industry may be found in technological innovations. Technological innovations may help retail store owners offer in-demand clothing lines or enhanced service for premium prices.

Keys to Success

To be successful in the retail store industry, competitors need to focus on hiring skilled employees. In other words, small businesses must employ and retain qualified and well-trained workers. Qualifications may not necessarily be in traditional schooling. However, experience with apparel coordination, technology, and customer service is necessitated to ensure that a guest has a memorable visit to a retail store.

SWOT Analysis

Strengths
- Management experience.
- Documented plans
- Themed retail concept
- Training program

Weakness
- Startup retail store.
- Untested business location.

Opportunities
- Community involvement
- Appeal to a wide variety of clientele.
- Location
- Brand building

Threats
- Local competitors
- Susceptible to economic downturn.

Competitive Analysis

Shop Here Retail Store is a "mom and pop" retail store in the Washington DC. area. The retail store was founded in 1984 and prides themselves on their 24hr availability (via online shopping opportunities). As for services, the retailer offers a high-end women's' clothing, focused on business casual, sports, and eveningwear. Based on a Google search, customers have had mixed reviews. Most reviews seemed satisfied with the retailer's clothing quality and service. However, some past customers complained that the cleanliness of the facility was lacking.

Organization and Management

Management Summary

John Smith, Sr., MBA., is the founder and CEO of ABC Retail store. He has started and managed numerous successful small retail stores over the last ten years. Retail stores started and managed, includes a high-end clothing store, athletic apparel location, and Walmart location. For each business, he was responsible for all aspects of the organization, from marketing to strategic planning.

Job Responsibilities

CEO:
- Create and execute marketing strategies for retail store growth.
- Align retail store strategies with the vision statement.
- Negotiating contracts with vendors.
- Ensure legal compliance for the retail store.
- Continually examine the firm's external environment for new market opportunities.

General Manager:
- Control inventory to ensure optimal levels are attained.
- Manage day-to-day operations of the retail store.
- Assist stockers and apparel coordinators during high volume times.
- Interview and hire new employees.
- Assist in the onboarding process for new employees.

Organizational Chart

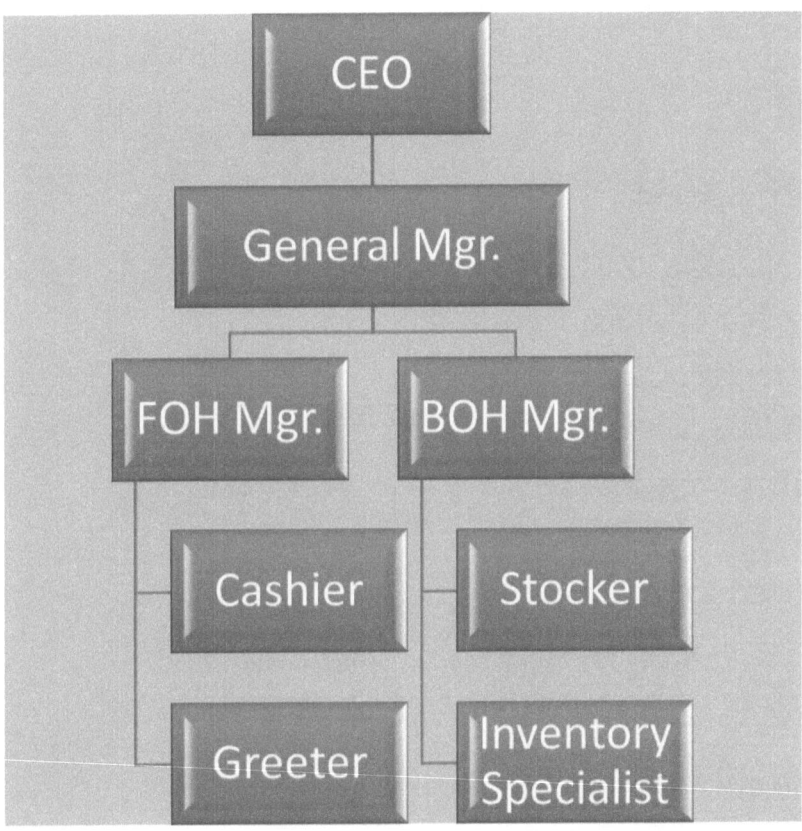

Marketing

Marketing Objectives and Keys to Success

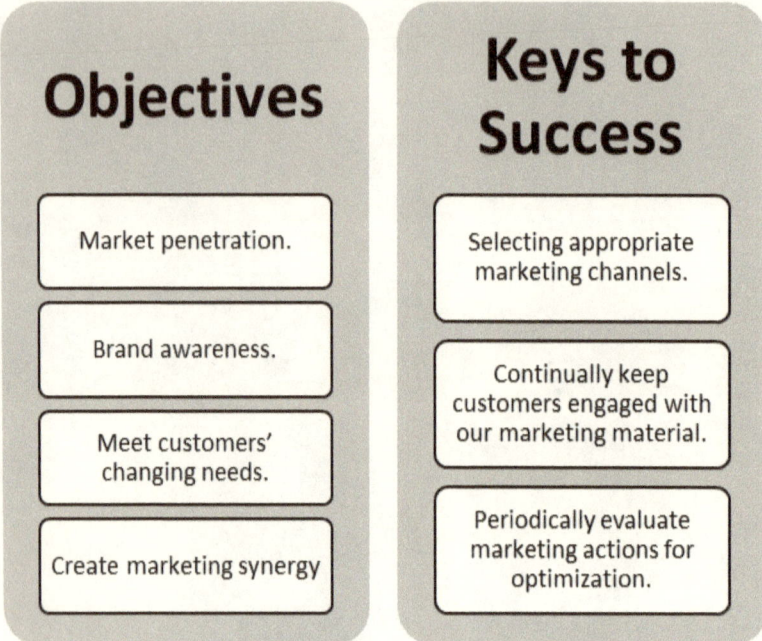

Traditional Marketing

Our first traditional marketing channel will include a professionally designed sign for the front of the retail store. This sign will include our retail store name, logo, and slogan. Further, prominent colors will include black, gold, and white. The objective of the signage is to let potential customers know our retail store's theme and possible products offered.

Internet Marketing

The importance of a professionally designed website cannot be understated. To exploit this opportunity, XYZ Retail store will create and maintain a website and Yelp listing. The objective of the strategy is to effectively communicate our retail store's theme and highlight our high-end product select.

Social Media Marketing

ABC Retail store's social media advertising will include Instagram, Twitter, and Facebook. Using a three-source approach to social media will ensure our message reaches a broad audience, which will include our target market. Also, several potential customers will receive an advertising message on multiple social media outlets. This should exceed the needed repetition of our message to a broad audience as well as our target market. The marketing message will focus on our retail store products offered and possible weekly specials.

Financial Projections

Financial Assumptions

Our financial projections have several assumptions based on research and management's expectation of potential sales and costs.

- All financial projections are based on management and or owner(s) professional expectations of sales and expenses for the foreseeable future.

- In the first 12 months, sales should increase by approximately 5% each month. In months 13 to 24, sales growth should slow to approximately .3% per month. For years three through five, sales are expected to grow by 4.5%.

- The cost of goods or variable costs are expected to be approximately 30.21% of total sales.

- The initial advertising budget will be $7,5000. Advertising is projected to increase by approximately 1% per year. This is to ensure maximum utilization of the firm's property and equipment.

- Cost projections were calculated using a common size model. This practice is typical for financial modeling.

- The tax rate was assumed to be 20%. Fluctuation in the tax rate will have a direct impact on net profits.

- The initial funding needed is 1,500,000. An increase/decrease in amount will impact the net present value and internal rate of return.

- The starting cash balance needed is $125,000 for working capital.

- A cash account was used to balance assets with liabilities and equity.

Financial Summary

The financial projections are based on market research and empirical examination of the local retail store industry. For the next year, we project revenues of approximately $456,793. The estimated expense costs will be $217,330. After taxes, we estimate a net profit of $239,463. This leads to a profit margin of approximately 52.4%. As our brand continues to grow, second-year progression is anticipated to yield a net income of approximately $311,363. Within five years, net income should exceed $348,722.

Startup Costs

Startup Costs	
Category	**Estimate**
Equity Investment	1,000,000.00
Loan	500,000.00
Initial Build Out	900,000
Working Capital	125,000.00
Section: Equipment	
Retail store Equipment (General)	75,000.00
FOH Inventory	35,000.00
BOH Equipment	40,000.00
Sub Total	150,000.00
Section: Operations	
Inventory	95,000.00
Supplies	150,000.00
Décor	28,000.00
Sub Total	273,000.00

Section: Office Equipment	
Office Equipment	25,000.00
Furniture	12,000.00
Sub Total	37,000.00
Section: Other	
Misc. Licenses	15,000.00
Sub Total	15,000.00
Total	1,500,000.00

Daily Revenues

Revenue Generators							
Daily Sales	% Sales	Num.	Price	Cost	Profit	Total Rev.	Total Cost
Shirts	40%	90	35.00	14.00	21.00	3,150.00	1260
Pants	40%	90	40.00	16.00	24.00	3,600.00	1440
Access.	40%	120	15.00	6.00	9.00	1,800.00	720
					Total	11,978	4,655

Labor

Labor				
Employee	Number	Rate	Monthly Hours	Total Pay
Salary		n/a	n/a	4,500
Manager	1	25.00	172	4,300
Employees	18	18.00	172	55,728

			Total	60,028

Monthly Fixed Costs

Monthly Fixed Costs	
Monthly Costs	**Monthly Total**
Rent	15,000
Utilities	1,580
Office Expenses	780
Insurance	400
Accounting/legal	250
Advertising	7500
Other	650
Monthly Total	26,160

Growth Rates

Growth Rates	
Growth Rate Sales 2 & 3	3.50%
Growth Rate Sales 4 & 5	1.50%
Growth Rate Cost of Goods	1.50%
Growth Rate Salary	1.50%
Growth Rate Labor	3.00%
Growth Advertising	1.00%
Growth Office	1.00%
Growth Utility	1.00%
Growth Legal	1.00%
Growth Insurance	1.00%
Growth Other	1.00%

Misc. Information

Misc. Information	
Tax Rate	20%
Cost of Capital	10%

Loan Payment Calculations

Loan Information	
Loan Amount	(500,000.00)
Interest Rate	7%
Term	25
Payment	$3,533.90

Profit and Loss Quarter 1

Pro Forma Income Statement Year 1 Quarter 1				
	Month 1	Month 2	Month 3	Quarter 1
Revenues	192,941	198,729	204,691	596,361
COGS	57,145	58,859	60,625	176,629
Gross Profit	135,796	139,870	144,066	419,732
Expenses				
Salary	4,500	4,500	4,500	13,500
Labor	60,028	60,028	60,028	180,084
Advertising	7,500	7,500	7,500	22,500
Office Expen.	780	803	828	2,411
Rent	15,000	15,000	15,000	45,000
Utilities	1,580	1,627	1,676	4,884
Legal / Account	250	250	250	750
Insurance	400	400	400	1,200
Depreciation	11,667	11,667	11,667	35,000

Other	650	650	650	1,950
Total Expenses	102,355	102,425	102,498	307,279
EBIT	33,441	37,445	41,568	112,454
Interest Expense	2,917	2,913	2,909	8,739
EBT	30,525	34,532	38,658	103,715
Taxes	6,105	6,906	7,732	20,743
Net Income	24,420	27,625	30,927	82,972

Profit and Loss Quarter 2

Pro Forma Income Statement Year 1 Quarter 2				
Income Statement	Month 4	Month 5	Month 6	Quarter 2
Revenues	210,832	217,157	223,671	651,660
COGS	62,444	64,317	66,247	193,007
Gross Profit	148,388	152,840	157,425	458,653
Expenses				
Salary	4,500	4,500	4,500	13,500
Labor	60,028	60,028	60,028	180,084
Advertising	7,500	7,500	7,500	22,500
Office Expen.	828	878	904	2,610
Rent	15,000	15,000	15,000	45,000
Utilities	1,676	1,778	1,832	5,286

Legal / Account	250	250	250	750
Insurance	400	400	400	1,200
Depreciation	11,667	11,667	11,667	35,000
Other	650	650	650	1,950
Total Expenses	102,498	102,651	102,731	307,880
EBIT	45,890	50,189	54,694	150,773
Interest Expense	2,906	2,902	2,898	8,706
EBT	42,984	47,287	51,796	142,067
Taxes	8,597	9,457	10,359	28,413
Net Income	34,387	37,829	41,437	113,653

Profit and Loss Quarter 3

Pro Forma Income Statement Year 1 Quarter 3			
Income Statement	**Month 7**	**Month 8**	**Month 9**	**Quarter 3**
Revenues	230,382	237,293	244,412	712,087
COGS	68,234	70,281	72,389	210,904
Gross Profit	162,148	167,012	172,022	501,182
Expenses				
Salary	4,500	4,500	4,500	13,500
Labor	60,028	60,028	60,028	180,084
Advertising	7,500	7,500	7,500	22,500

Office Expen.	904	959	988	2,852
Rent	15,000	15,000	15,000	45,000
Utilities	1,832	1,943	2,001	5,776
Legal / Account	250	250	250	750
Insurance	400	400	400	1,200
Depreciation	11,667	11,667	11,667	35,000
Other	650	650	650	1,950
Total Expenses	102,731	102,897	102,984	308,612
EBIT	59,417	64,115	69,038	192,570
Interest Expense	2,895	2,891	2,887	8,673
EBT	56,522	61,224	66,151	183,897
Taxes	11,304	12,245	13,230	36,779
Net Income	45,218	48,979	52,921	147,118

Profit and Loss Quarter 4

Pro Forma Income Statement Year 1 Quarter 4				
Income Statement	**Month 10**	**Month 11**	**Month 12**	**Quarter 4**
Revenues	251,744	259,297	267,075	778,116
COGS	74,561	76,798	79,102	230,461
Gross Profit	177,183	182,499	187,974	547,655
Expenses				

Salary	4,500	4,500	4,500	13,500
Labor	60,028	60,028	60,028	180,084
Advertising	7,500	7,500	7,500	22,500
Office Expen.	988	1,048	1,080	3,116
Rent	15,000	15,000	15,000	45,000
Utilities	2,001	2,123	2,187	6,312
Legal / Account	250	250	250	750
Insurance	400	400	400	1,200
Depreciation	11,667	11,667	11,667	35,000
Other	650	650	650	1,950
Total Expenses	102,984	103,166	103,261	309,412
EBIT	74,199	79,332	84,712	238,243
Interest Expense	2,883	2,880	2,876	8,639
EBT	71,315	76,453	81,836	229,604
Taxes	14,263	15,291	16,367	45,921
Net Income	57,052	61,162	65,469	183,684

Income Statement

Pro Forma Income Statement - Base				
	Year 1	Year 2	Year 3	Year 4	Year 5
Revenues	2,738,224	3,266,320	3,380,641	3,431,351	3,482,821
COGS					

	811,001	967,412	981,923	996,652	1,011,601
Gross Profit	1,927,223	2,298,908	2,398,718	2,434,699	2,471,220
Expenses					
Salary	54,000	54,810	55,632	56,467	57,314
Labor	720,336	741,946	764,204	787,131	810,745
Advert.	90,000	90,900	91,809	92,727	93,654
Office Expenses	10,988	13,195	13,327	13,460	13,595
Rent	180,000	180,000	180,000	180,000	180,000
Utilities	22,258	26,729	26,996	27,266	27,538
Legal / Account	3,000	3,030	3,060	3,091	3,122
Insur.	4,800	4,848	4,896	4,945	4,995
Deprec.	140,000	237,500	168,150	124,020	117,090
Other	7,800	7,878	7,957	8,036	8,117
Total Expenses	1,233,182	1,360,836	1,316,032	1,297,143	1,316,169
EBIT	694,041	938,073	1,082,686	1,137,556	1,155,050
Interest Expense	34,758	34,205	33,612	32,976	32,294
Earnings before taxes	659,283	903,868	1,049,074	1,104,580	1,122,756
Taxes	131,857	180,774	209,815	220,916	224,551
Net Income	527,426	723,094	839,260	883,664	898,205

Balance Sheet

Balance Sheet - Pro Forma					
Assets	Year 1	Year 2	Year 3	Year 4	Year 5
Cash	867,202	1,821,416	2,821,905	3,822,085	4,830,119
Accts Receiv.	-	-	-	-	-
Invent.	67,583	80,618	81,827	83,054	84,300
Total Curr. Assets	934,785	1,902,034	2,903,732	3,905,139	4,914,419
PP&E	1,360,000	1,360,000	1,360,000	1,360,000	1,360,000
Less Deprec.	140,000	377,500	545,650	669,670	786,760
Net PP&E	1,220,000	982,500	814,350	690,330	573,240
Total Assets	2,154,785	2,884,534	3,718,082	4,595,469	5,487,659

Balance Sheet - Pro Forma					
Liabilities	Year 1	Year 2	Year 3	Year 4	Year 5
Accounts Pay	67,583	80,618	81,827	83,054	84,300
Notes Payable	2,896	2,850	2,801	2,748	2,691
Accruals	64,528	66,396	68,320	70,300	72,338
Total Current Liab.	135,008	149,864	152,948	156,102	159,329
Loans	492,351	484,149	475,354	465,923	456,681
Total Liab.	627,359	634,013	628,302	622,025	616,010
Common Stock	1,000,000	1,000,000	1,000,000	1,000,000	1,000,000
Retained Earnings	527,426	1,250,521	2,089,780	2,973,444	3,871,649

Total Com. Equity	1,527,426	2,250,521	3,089,780	3,973,444	4,871,649
Total Liab & Equity	2,154,785	2,884,534	3,718,082	4,595,469	5,487,659

Financial Ratios

Financial Ratios					
	Year 1	Year 2	Year 3	Year 4	Year 5
Return on Equity	34.53%	32.13%	27.16%	22.24%	18.44%
Return on Asset	24.48%	25.07%	22.57%	19.23%	16.37%
Current Ratio	6.92	12.69	18.99	25.02	30.84
Profit Margin	19.26%	22.14%	24.83%	25.75%	25.79%
Net Present Value	9,050,885				
IRR	83.40%				

Funding Request

To start operations, funding of $1,500,000 in debt or equity from a bank or investor is required. Debt funding is expected to have a term of 15 to 20 years with an interest rate between 8% to 10%. Principle and interest payments will be made monthly, using profits from the business. For investors, a negotiated percentage of ownership in the retail store will be offered. In addition, after the second year of profitability, investors will be compensated through semi-annually dividend payments from business cash flows.

Received funds will be used as follows:

Startup Costs	
Category	**Estimate**
Equity Investment	1,000,000.00
Loan	500,000.00
Initial Build Out	900,000
Working Capital	125,000.00
Section: Equipment	
Retail store Equipment (General)	75,000.00
FOH Equipment	35,000.00
BOH Equipment	40,000.00
Sub Total	150,000.00
Section: Operations	
Inventory	95,000.00
Supplies	150,000.00
Décor	28,000.00
Sub Total	273,000.00
Section: Office Equipment	

Office Equipment	25,000.00
Furniture	12,000.00
Sub Total	37,000.00
Section: Other	
Misc. Licenses	15,000.00
Sub Total	15,000.00
Total	**1,500,000.00**

Paul Borosky

XXX Rachelle Dr. - Sanford, FL. 32771 - (321) 948-**** –
Paulb@Qualitybusinessplan.com

Professional Experience

Quality Business Plan — **Business Consulting – Business Plan Writing**

Sanford, Fl. / Online

October 2010 - Present

* Prepared pro forma financial statements.
* Research various industries for trends, revenues, and growth projections.
* Calculate various financial ratios such as Return on Equity and Current Ratio.
* Write business plans for current and prospective businesses.

XXX High school — **Entrepreneurship / Microsoft Office / Computer Programming Instructor**

Durham, NC.

August, 2014 – October, 2016

* Prepare lesson plans for Excel, Word, Visual Basic, and other classes.
* Assign and grade various assignments.
* Provide in-depth student feedback in residential settings.
* Assist students through numerous stages of learning.

XXX College — **Resident and Online Adjunct Finance / Entrepreneurship Instructor**

Ocala, Fl.

June, 2013 – December 2016

* Prepare lesson plans for residential class.
* Assign and grade various finance assignments.
* Provide in-depth student feedback in residential and online settings.
* Assist students through numerous stages of learning.

* Subject Matter Expert – Created and Designed college level finance classes.

Walt Disney World Resorts Supervisor
Orlando, Fl.
pace environment.
April, 2011-Jan, 2013
service to guest.

basics.

example and instruction.

Quick Service Food -

* Prepared guest meals in fast

* Display exceptional customer

* Daily practice Disney's leader

* Lead other cast members by

Education

Northcentral University	DBA, Management – Doctoral Candidate Ongoing
Webster University	Finance – 21 Master level credit hours 2011
Webster University (MBA)	Masters in Business Administration 2010
Barry University	Bachelors in Professional Studies with specialization in Administration 2009
Seminole State College	AA Degree 2002

Training and Skills

Blackboard Learning System	Rasmussen College	2016
Microsoft PowerPoint Certified	Certiport	2016
Microsoft Excel Certified	Certiport	2016
Microsoft Word Certified	Certiport	2015
Canvas Learning System	Voyager High School	2015
NC Department of Education License	Temporary Professional Educator's	2014
Angel Learning System	Rasmussen College	2013

Fl. Department of Education	Statement of Status of Eligibility –
Business (grades 6-12)	2013
Online Faculty Training	Rasmussen College
	2013
Salesforce	Training for Salesforce software

Retail Store Business Plan Template (Includes Market Research!)

Executive Summary

Retail Store Summary: (Retail store Name) is a (Business legal structure: limited liability corporation, sole proprietor, corporation) located in City, State. Our firm offers (products and services offered).

Our (type of retail store) business specializes in (what will your retail store do best?).

(Name of a retail store) utilizes a (pricing strategy: best value, low price, premium) pricing model to ensure a fair price is offered to our customers. Our hours of operation are from (8:00 AM to 10 PM), (seven days a week, Monday – Friday, etc.). Our staff size is (four), including the owner. An important key to success in sustaining our retail store is to (important action that your retail store needs to take in order to succeed).

Target Market: Our primary target market will be (expected target market) between the ages of (age) to (age).

Financial Highlights: The financial projections are based on market research and empirical examination of the local retail store industry. For the next year, we project revenues of approximately $(a dollar amount). The estimated expense costs will be $(a dollar amount). After taxes, we estimate a net profit of $(a dollar amount). This leads to a profit margin of approximately (percent)%.

Funding Request: To start operations, funding of $(a dollar amount) in debt or equity from a bank or investor is required. Debt funding is expected to have a term of (15) to (20) years with an interest rate between (rate)% to (rate)%. Principle and interest payments will be made monthly, using profits from the business. For investors, a negotiated percentage of ownership in the retail store will be offered. In addition, investors will be compensated through (when will dividends be paid: quarterly, semi-annually, etc.) dividend payments from business cash flows.

Retail store Description

Retail store Summary

(Retail store Name) will be a (business legal structure: corporate, sole proprietor, limited liability corporation, corporate, etc.) located at (address) in (city, state). The business owner will be (your name). Our (type of retail store: café, casual dining, etc.) will offer on (product items offered). Our hours of operation will be from (hours of operations).

Competitive Advantages

(Name of Retail store) will have specific competitive advantages once our firm starts operations. First, (your main competitive advantage).

A second competitive advantage would be (second competitive advantage).

Product Description

(Product 1)
Our (product 1) will (describe product).

(Product 2)
Our (product 2) will (describe product).

(Product 3)
Our (product 3) will (describe product).

Pricing Strategy

Our pricing structure will be focused on a (low cost, best value, premium) pricing. The strategy was selected because (explain why you selected this pricing strategy).

Business Models

Operations:

Our operational structure will (describe how your retail store will operate).

Hours of Operations:

Our hours of operations business model will be structured to ensure our customers' needs are met at a convenient time. From this, our organization will be open from (hours of operation).

Location

As previously stated, our location will be at (retail store address). The proposed location size will be about (number) square feet. Approximately (percent) of the area will be dedicated to (what will be the main use of your facility). The rest of the area will be dedicated to (what else will your location be used for?).

As for competition, this area has about (number) competitors, offering similar products within a (number) square mile range.

Future Plans

Within the next (number) months, our firm will (discuss your future plans).

Business Objectives and Time Line

1 - 3 Months

- o Objective 1
- o Objective 2
- o Objective 3
- o Objective 4

3 – 6 Months

- o Objective 1
- o Objective 2
- o Objective 3

6 – 12 Months

- o Objective 1
- o Objective 2
- o Objective 3

Mission Statement

(Enter your mission statement here)

Vision Statement

(Enter your vision statement here)

Value Statement

- o Value 1
- o Value 2
- o Value 3
- o Value 4

Keys to Success

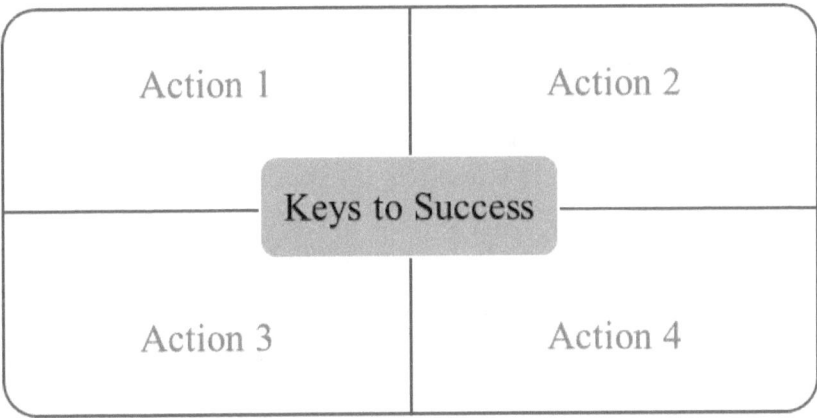

Target Market

Primary Target Market

Our primary target market will be (describe target market), specifically (male or female) between the ages of (age) to (age). This demographic was selected because (talk about why you selected this target market).

Secondary Target Market

As for the secondary target market, this will be (describe target market), specifically (male or female) between the ages of (age) to (age). This demographic was selected because (talk about why you selected this target market).

Target Market Growth

Based on research from (where did you get the target market growth information), the current target market population in the area is about (number) (individuals or businesses).

The (name of the source for researched information) has noted that the city's population has increased by (percent)% annually over the last (number) years. Based on this factor, our retail store expects a similar growth rate for the next (number) years. From this, the target market formulation will be (number) within the next (number) months. In two years, our target market population will expand to (number) (people or businesses).

Retail store Market Analysis

In this market analysis, the industry, economy, and overall risk for the company will be analyzed for a better understanding of our external environment.

Industry: Retail Store Industry.
The retail store industry is immensely popular in the US. Total sales for the industry in 2018 were about 39 billion. These sales were generated from over 265,000 million establishments. Multinational corporations account for a large portion of sales. However, single-unit owners capture the numerous niche markets in the industry. From this review, entrepreneurs with a creative twist to operating a retail store may carve out significant revenues from the industry.

Growth:
Over the last five years, the retail store industry has experienced approximately 3% growth annually. Future growth in the retail store industry is expected to be approximately 2% annually, which is adjusted for inflation[2].

Trends:
Growth in the retail store industry has been steady for the last several years. However, recently, some chain retail store operators have experienced above-normal increased revenues. An important segment of this growth is delivery and same-day delivery.

Threats:

The retail store industry does have specific threats. As the economy continues to grow, the labor market will continually tighten. This will challenge retail store owners in attracting and retaining qualified workers. A second threat to the industry is government regulations. Retail stores need to comply with various national, regional and local regulations related to pay, safety and labor rules. Additional regulations may further strain profit margins.

Detailed SWOT Analysis

SWOT analysis:

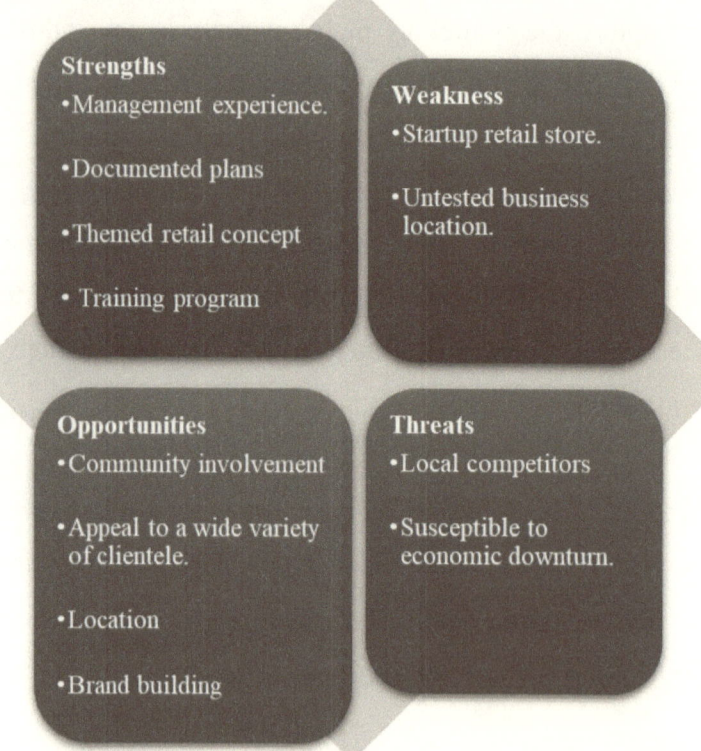

Strengths
- Management experience.
- Documented plans
- Themed retail concept
- Training program

Weakness
- Startup retail store.
- Untested business location.

Opportunities
- Community involvement
- Appeal to a wide variety of clientele.
- Location
- Brand building

Threats
- Local competitors
- Susceptible to economic downturn.

Competitive Analysis

(Competitor 1)
(Competitor 1) is located (address). This is about (number) miles from our proposed location. The retail store offers (product items). Based on a (Google or Facebook) search, important information was obtained. Previous customers, based on reviews, had mostly (good or bad) reviews. Specifically, the main area discussed was (what was most talked about on Google or Facebook reviews). As a result of the (Google or Facebook) reviews, the retail store currently has a (number) star rating.

(Competitor 2)
(Competitor 1) is located (address). This is about (number) miles from our proposed location. The retail store offers (product items). Based on a (Google or Facebook) search, important information was obtained. Previous customers, based on reviews, had mostly (good or bad) reviews. Specifically, the main area discussed was (what was most talked about on Google or Facebook reviews). As a result of the (Google or Facebook) reviews, the retail store currently has a (number) star rating.

(Competitor 3)
(Competitor 1) is located (address). This is about (number) miles from our proposed location. The retail store offers (product items). Based on a (Google or Facebook) search, important information was obtained. Previous customers, based on reviews, had mostly (good or bad) reviews. Specifically, the main area discussed was (what was most talked about on Google or Facebook reviews). As a result of the (Google or Facebook) reviews, the retail store currently has a (number) star rating.

Organization and Management

Management Summary

(Owner name) is the founder and CEO of (retail store name), which is a (business legal structure: sole proprietor, limited liability retail store, partnership, corporation). (He or she) has (number) years' experience in the retail store industry. From this experience, (owner name) has developed specialized critical skills needed to lead and manage this endeavor.

Job Responsibilities

CEO:

- Create and execute all business strategies for growth.
- Align retail store strategies with mission and vision statements.
- Negotiating contracts with vendors and suppliers.
- Ensure all laws are followed in the retail store.
- Continually examine the firm's external environment for new opportunities.

Manager:

- Control inventory to ensure optimal levels are achieved.
- Manage day-to-day operations of the retail store.
- Help employees during high volume times.
- Interview and hire new employees.
- Assist in the onboarding process for new employees.

Ast. Manager:

- Conduct initial interviews for hiring.

- Floor operations.

- Responsible for taking inventory.

- Opening and closing retail store.

- Sign off on all side work for the front and back of the house.

Organizational Chart

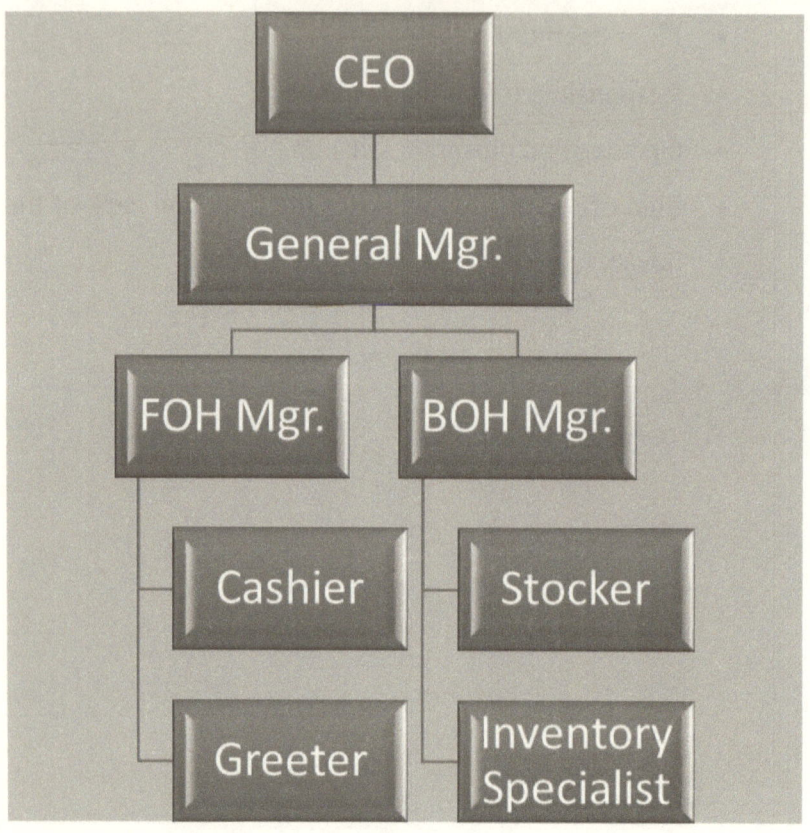

Marketing

Marketing Objectives and Keys to Success

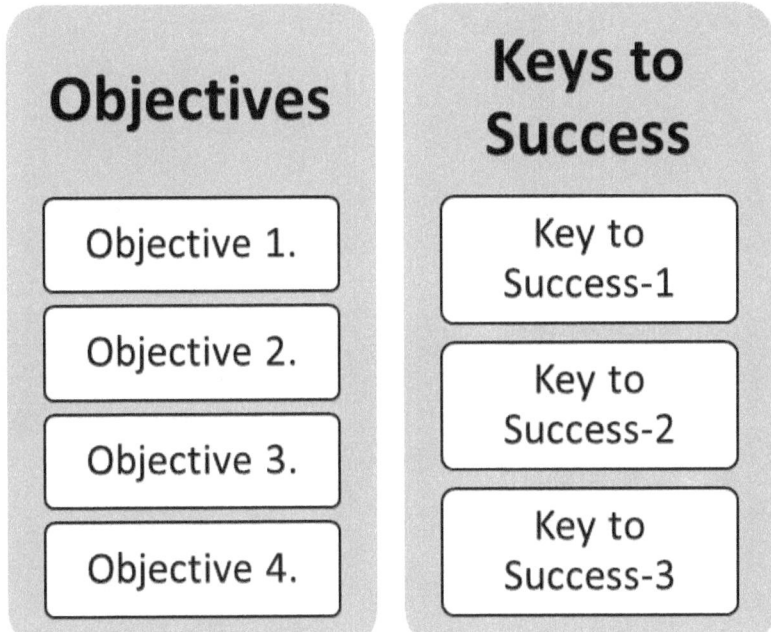

Traditional Marketing

Our first traditional marketing channel will include a (discuss your advertising ideas related to mailers, building signs, etc.).

Internet Marketing

The importance of a professionally designed website cannot be understated. To exploit this opportunity, (retail store name) will create and maintain a website with links to our social media channels. The objective of the strategy is to effectively communicate the product line that we offer.

Social Media Marketing

(Name of a retail store) its social media advertising will include Instagram, Twitter, and Facebook. Using a three-channel approach to social media will ensure our message reaches a broad audience, which will include our target market.

Financial Projections

Financial Assumptions

Our financial projections have several assumptions based on research and management's expectation of potential sales and costs.

- All financial projections are based on management and or owner(s) professional expectations of sales and expenses for the foreseeable future.

- In the first 12 months, sales should increase by approximately (percent)% each month. In months 13 to 24, sales growth should slow to approximately (percent)% per month. For years three through five, sales are expected to grow by (percent)%.

- The cost of goods or variable costs are expected to be approximately (percent)% of total sales.

- The initial advertising budget will be $(dollar amount). Advertising is projected to increase by approximately (percent)% per year. This is to ensure maximum utilization of the firm's assets.

- Cost projections were calculated using a common size model. This practice is typical for financial modeling.

- The tax rate was assumed to be (percent)%. Fluctuation in the tax rate will have a direct impact on net profits.

- The initial funding needed is $(dollar amount). An increase/decrease in amount will impact the net present value and internal rate of return.

- Starting cash balance needed is $(dollar amount) for working capital.

134

- A cash account was used to balance assets with liabilities and equity.

Financial Summary

The financial projections are based on market research and empirical examination of the retail store industry. For the next year, we project revenues of approximately $(dollar amount). The estimated expense costs will be $(dollar amount). After taxes, we estimate a net profit of $(dollar amount). This leads to a profit margin of approximately (percent)%. As our brand continues to grow, second-year progression is anticipated to yield a net income of approximately $(dollar amount). Within five years, net income should exceed $(dollar amount).

Startup Costs

Startup Costs	
Category	Estimate
Equity Investment	
Loan	
Initial Build Out	
Working Capital	
Section: Equipment	
Sub Total	
Section: Operations	
Sub Total	

Section: Office Equipment	
Sub Total	
Section: Other	
Sub Total	
Total	

Daily Revenues

Average Daily Sales						
Revenue Generators						
Daily Sales	Num.	Price	Cost	Profit	Total Rev.	Total Cost
Section 1						
Item 1						
Item 2						
Item 3						
Section 2						
Item 1						
Item 2						
Item 3						
				Total		

Labor

Labor				
Employee	Number	Rate	Monthly Hours	Total Pay
Salary				

Manager				
Employees				
			Total	

Monthly Fixed Costs

Monthly Fixed Costs	
Monthly Costs	**Monthly Total**
Rent	
Utilities	
Office Expenses	
Insurance	
Accounting/legal	
Advertising	
Other	
Monthly Total	

Growth Rates

Growth Rates	
Growth Rate Sales 2 & 3	%
Growth Rate Sales 4 & 5	%
Growth Rate Cost of Goods	%
Growth Rate Salary	%
Growth Rate Labor	%
Growth Advertising	%
Growth Office	%
Growth Utility	%
Growth Legal	%
Growth Insurance	%
Growth Other	%

Misc. Information

Misc. Information	
Tax Rate	%
Cost of Capital	%

Loan Payment Calculations

Loan Information	
Loan Amount	
Interest Rate	%
Term	
Payment	

Profit and Loss Quarter 1

Pro Forma Income Statement Year 1 Quarter 1				
	Month 1	Month 2	Month 3	Quarter 1
Revenues				
COGS				
Gross Profit				
Expenses				
Salary				
Labor				
Advertising				
Office Expen.				
Rent				
Utilities				
Legal / Account				
Insurance				
Depreciation				
Other				
Total Expenses				

138

EBIT				
Interest Expense				
EBT				
Taxes				
Net Income				

Profit and Loss Quarter 2

Pro Forma Income Statement Year 1 Quarter 2				
	Month 1	Month 2	Month 3	Quarter 1
Revenues				
COGS				
Gross Profit				
Expenses				
Salary				
Labor				
Advertising				
Office Expen.				
Rent				
Utilities				
Legal / Account				
Insurance				
Depreciation				
Other				
Total Expenses				
EBIT				
Interest Expense				

EBT			
Taxes			
Net Income			

Profit and Loss Quarter 3

Pro Forma Income Statement Year 1 Quarter 3			
	Month 1	Month 2	Month 3	Quarter 1
Revenues				
COGS				
Gross Profit				
Expenses				
Salary				
Labor				
Advertising				
Office Expen.				
Rent				
Utilities				
Legal / Account				
Insurance				
Depreciation				
Other				
Total Expenses				
EBIT				
Interest Expense				
EBT				
Taxes				
Net Income				

Profit and Loss Quarter 4

Pro Forma Income Statement Year 1 Quarter 4				
	Month 1	Month 2	Month 3	Quarter 1
Revenues				
COGS				
Gross Profit				
Expenses				
Salary				
Labor				
Advertising				
Office Expen.				
Rent				
Utilities				
Legal / Account				
Insurance				
Depreciation				
Other				
Total Expenses				
EBIT				
Interest Expense				
EBT				
Taxes				
Net Income				

Income Statement

Pro Forma Income Statement Year 1 Quarter 1

	Year 1	Year 2	Year 3	Year 4
Revenues				
COGS				
Gross Profit				
Expenses				
Salary				
Labor				
Advertising				
Office Expen.				
Rent				
Utilities				
Legal / Account				
Insurance				
Depreciation				
Other				
Total Expenses				
EBIT				
Interest Expense				
EBT				
Taxes				
Net Income				

Balance Sheet

Balance Sheet - Pro Forma					
Assets	Year 1	Year 2	Year 3	Year 4	Year 5
Cash					
Accts Receiv.					

Invent.					
Total Curr. Assets					
PP&E					
Less Deprec.					
Net PP&E					
Total Assets					

Balance Sheet - Pro Forma					
Liabilities	Year 1	Year 2	Year 3	Year 4	Year 5
Accounts Pay					
Notes Payable					
Accruals					
Total Current Liab.					
Loans					
Total Liab.					
Common Stock					
Retained Earnings					
Total Com. Equity					
Total Liab & Equity					

Financial Ratios

Financial Ratios					
	Year 1	Year 2	Year 3	Year 4	Year 5
Return on					

Equity					
Return on Asset					
Current Ratio					
Profit Margin					
Net Present Value					
IRR					

Funding Request

To start operations, funding of $(dollar amount) in debt or equity from a bank or investor is required. Debt funding is expected to have a term of (number) to (number) years with an interest rate between (percent)% to (percent)%. Principle and interest payments will be made monthly, using profits from the business. For investors, a negotiated percentage of ownership in the retail store will be offered. In addition, investors will be compensated through (monthly, quarter, semi-annually) dividend payments from business cash flows.

Received funds will be used as follows:

Startup Costs	
Category	Estimate
Equity Investment	
Loan	
Initial Build Out	
Working Capital	
Section: Equipment	
Sub Total	
Section: Operations	
Sub Total	
Section: Office Equipment	

Sub Total	
Section: Other	
Sub Total	
Total